BLACK BASEBALL

BLACK BASEBALL

A History of African–Americans & the National Game

Kyle McNary

PRC

ACKNOWLEDGMENTS

The publisher wishes to thank all those who kindly supplied photographs for this book, as follows:

© Duomo/CORBIS for front cover, and pages 101 (top and bottom), 102 (left) and 105;

National Baseball Hall of Fame Library, Cooperstown, NY for pages 2, 36 and 164;

Larry Lester (NoirTech Research, Inc.) for pages: 5, 8, 10 (bottom), 11, 12, 13, 15 (top and bottom), 16, 17 (top and bottom), 18, 19 (right), 20 (top), 21 (bottom), 22 (left and right), 23, 30, 32 (top), 33 (top right and bottom), 34, 38, 39 (top and bottom), 40, 42, 43, 44 (bottom), 46, 48, 50 (top and bottom), 53 (top), 54 (right), 56, 57, 58, 59, 78, 79 (bottom), 80 (bottom), 108, 109, 111, 112, 113, 115, 116, 117, 118, 119 (top and bottom), 122, 123, 124, 125 (bottom), 126, 128 (bottom), 129, 130 (bottom), 131, 132, 133, 136, 138, 139, 141, 144, 146, 147, 148, 149, 151, 152, 153, 156, 158, 160, 161, 163, 165 and 167, and back cover (top);

National Baseball Hall of Fame Library, Cooperstown, NY/NBLA for pages 6 (bottom) and 76 (bottom);

Collection of Kyle McNary for pages 7, 21 (top), 27 (bottom), 28, 29, 32 (bottom), 33 (top left), 35 (top), 37 (top), 44 (top), 45, 49, 53 (bottom), 61, 106 (top), 114, 121, 127, 130 (top), 134, 135, 145 and 154;

National Baseball Hall of Fame Library, Cooperstown, NY/© Photofile for pages 9 (top), 55, 62 (top), 63, 65, 68 (left), 69, 70, 72 (top and bottom), 73 (top), 74, 75 (bottom), 80 (top), 81 (bottom), 82, 84, 88, 89, 91 (top), 92, 95, 96, 98 (top and bottom), 99 (bottom), 100, 102 (right), 103 and 104;

© Bettmann/CORBIS for pages 6 (top), 9 (bottom), 47, 51, 52, 62 (bottom), 64 (top and bottom), 66 (top and bottom), 67 (left and right), 68 (right), 71, 73 (bottom), 75 (top), 76 (top), 77, 79 (top), 81 (top), 85, 86, 91 (bottom), 94, 140, 142, 143, 155, 159, 168 and 172;

Kyle McNary (Collection: Mike Ellis) for pages 10 (top) and 19 (left);

Kyle McNary (Collection: Breedlove) for pages 20 (bottom), 25, 31 and 37 (bottom);

Kyle McNary (Collection: Bertha Historical Society) for pages 26 and 35 (bottom), and back cover (bottom);

Kyle McNary (Collection: Brown) for page 27 (top);

Kyle McNary (Collection: Minnesota Historical Society) for pages 54 (left) and 128 (top);

© Neal Preston/CORBIS for page 83;

National Baseball Hall of Fame Library, Cooperstown, NY/Steven Schwab/NBLA for page 99 (top);

Kyle McNary (Collection: Steve Faytis) for pages 106 (bottom) and 107;

Kyle McNary (Collection: Rich Maxson) for page 125 (top).

Produced in 2003 by
PRC Publishing Ltd,
The Chrysalis Building
Bramley Road, London W10 6SP

An imprint of **Chrysalis** Books Group plc

This edition published in 2003
Distributed in the U.S. and Canada by:
Sterling Publishing Co., Inc.
387 Park Avenue South
New York, NY 10016

© 2003 PRC Publishing Ltd

ISBN 1 85648 694 X

Printed and bound in Malaysia

Contents

Introduction

It's been said that to understand America you need to understand baseball, for it mirrors the society as a whole. James Earl Jones in the movie *Field of Dreams* said it best: "America has rolled by like an army of steamrollers. It has been erased like a blackboard, rebuilt, and erased again, but baseball has marked the time. This field, this game, it's a part of our past. It reminds us of all that once was good and could be again."

For decades, families made their way into Major League and Minor League ballparks across the United States, sat in their seats, and looked out across the baseball field. What they saw was a visual symphony of colors: beautiful green grass, deep dark brown dirt, and graceful athletes clad in clean uniforms of blue, red, gray, and orange.

What many fans didn't overtly realize was that every one of these athletes had white skin, not bronze, brown, or black. Many baseball fans from the pre-Jackie Robinson era admit that their memories of those games are tainted with the knowledge that the playing fields, although aesthetically beautiful, were not level. If you had kinky hair and a brown tint to your face, you were not welcome, no matter how far you could hit the baseball, or how fast your fastball hummed. "It kind of makes all

those Major League teams, and all the records those men set seem diluted," one fan admitted.

Questions rush to mind: Would Babe Ruth have hit sixty home runs in 1927 if Willie Foster had been on the Washington Senators pitching staff instead of Tom Zachary who gave up the Babe's 22nd, 36th, and 60th dingers? Would Joe DiMaggio have hit in 56 straight games if "Satchel" Paige and Hilton Smith had been in the starting rotation of the Washington Senators instead of Ken Chase and Steve Sundra (6-18 and 9-13, respectively)? Would Hack Wilson have driven in 191 runs in 1930 if National League pitchers had included "Submarine" McDonald, Martin Dihigo, Sam Streeter, Ted Trent, and "Double Duty" Radcliffe? Or maybe Wilson would have driven in 191, but would he have led the league? Maybe Josh Gibson, Mule Suttles, or John Beckwith would have driven in 200!

The fact is nothing is solved when asking: what might have been? We can, however, appreciate the men of color who, when denied the opportunity to

Right: Reggie Jackson, one of baseball history's greatest sluggers, homered off men of every race, creed, and color.

Far right: Hoss Walker played several positions and managed during his 30-year career, a common feat in the Negro Leagues.

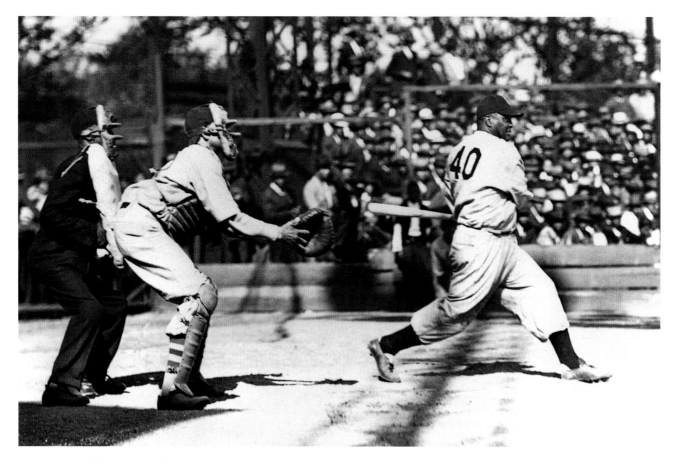

Above: Raleigh "Biz" Mackey caught for almost 30 years, and was a rare power-hitting switch-hitter.

play in the Major and Minor Leagues back in the 1880s, formed their own teams and own leagues and created a glory all their own. For every Lou Gehrig in the Majors, there was a Buck Leonard in the Negro Leagues; for every Ty Cobb, there was an Oscar Charleston; and for every Mel Ott, there was a Turkey Stearnes. It was these men, who by virtue of their love and dedication to baseball, blazed the trail that Jackie Robinson followed in integrated Organized Baseball. And once Robinson entered the Majors in 1947 with the Brooklyn Dodgers, the job of integration was far from complete. Men like Larry Doby, Joe Black, Hank Aaron, and Elston Howard helped carry Robinson's torch and, they in turn, passed it along to men like Bob Gibson, Frank Robinson, Billy Williams, and Roberto Clemente. Every generation produced proud men willing to carry the load, methodically breaking down each barrier one by one. There had to be a first black pitcher, first black catcher, first black Most Valuable Player, first black Yankee, first black manager, first black general manager, and maybe someday a first black baseball owner or commissioner.

Modern stars like Barry Bonds, Sammy Sosa, Ozzie Smith, Tony Gwynn, and Pedro Martinez are very aware of the black baseball heroes of the past that helped them reach great heights. They have openly expressed their gratitude to Curt Flood, Jackie Robinson, and hundreds of Negro Leaguers who paid the dues—the expensive and sometimes painful dues.

Black Baseball is a journey of sorts, that starts with the men of the Civil War era, who whittled their own bats and played on cow pastures, follows Rube Foster's successful Negro National League of the 1920s through the depression years when a team might go bankrupt if it rained two days in a row, past the attendance boom of the war years, across the bridge of integration, and comes to a restful stop in the present day. Now, great black baseball players can make more in a three-game-series than Josh Gibson made in a lifetime and their talents are on display for the entire world to see.

Black Baseball will introduce you to men you have never heard of, and will add depth to your knowledge of men you thought you knew. There is still progress to be made in baseball, and bigotry still rears its ugly head when we think we've licked it, but it's nice to know how far we've come; that our national pastime still grabs our attention and touches our soul. Kids of all races still dream of playing this wonderful game.

Above: Outfielder Lou Brock brought the stolen base to a level never seen before in the Major Leagues.

Below: Bobby Bonds, father of current great Barry Bonds, combined speed and power in the 1960s like few before or since.

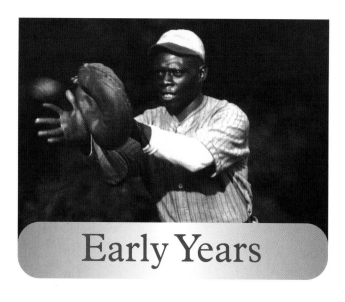

Early Years

Baseball, as we know it, is as old as America itself. Since the pilgrims arrived in the 1500s, kids have been swinging sticks at everything from rocks to rolled-up socks. Can you think of anything more natural for an American youngster to do than run, throw, and hit?

It's believed that Dr. Oliver Wendell Holmes played baseball while attending Harvard in 1829 and in 1833 some men in Philadelphia formed the Olympic Town Ball Club, one of the first traveling baseball teams. Alexander Cartwright (not Abner Doubleday as many believe) became the father of modern baseball in the 1840s when he laid out the first "official" baseball field and rules—quite astonishingly close to what we have today. Cartwright formed a team made up of his New York City buddies, called them the Knickerbockers, and built their home field on Elysian Fields (now Hoboken, N.J.). In 1849, Cartwright hit the road with his team and several covered wagons filled with equipment, and taught the game all across the continent. He was, like Johnny Appleseed, planting the seed of baseball interest. Several years later Cartwright sailed to Hawaii and spent the final years of his life teaching the game to the natives.

By the 1850s baseball had become popular across the country and the first documented college game pitted Amherst against Williams College. No gloves were worn, no catcher's equipment used, and the game ended in an Amherst win by about forty runs! From the earliest days of American baseball, black players showed a passion and talent for the game. Black players could be found in some of the earliest college and semipro teams across the

country. Welday Walker, who went on to even greater diamond exploits, honed his skills with Oberlin College in Ohio in the late 1870s.

At the outset of the Civil War, New York City boasted more than 60 organized semipro teams, but the war cut that number in half as many of the best players took up arms against their own countrymen. It was during the Civil War that baseball really took off in popularity as Union and Confederate camps found plenty of time between battles to play ball, and it became the pastime of choice among soldiers.

By 1869, the *New York Times* estimated the number of organized baseball clubs in America at more than 1,000. The top team that year and the first all-professional team was the 1869 Cincinnati Red Stockings who challenged all comers and went 57-0. After American slaves were freed following the Civil War, blacks started taking up the game in larger numbers and could be found playing with

Far left: Welday Walker (front row, center) with the integrated 1883 University of Michigan baseball team.

Below: Welday Walker (top row, second from right) and Moses Fleetwood Walker (middle row, far left), with the 1883 Toledo Blue Stockings of the Major Leagues.

many top semipro teams in the country, usually in the North.

According to Sol White's *Official Base Ball Guide*, the first all-black baseball team in the U.S. was organized in 1885. The team was a group of waiters from the Argyle Hotel in Babylon, New York, and were hired to entertain hotel guests. Players included third baseman Ben Holmes, first baseman A. Randolph, second baseman Ben Boyd, shortstop William Eggleston, catcher Guy Day, pitchers George Parego, Frank Harris, and R. Mortin, and outfielders Milton Dabney and Charles Nichols. The players spoke gibberish on the field, which they hoped would sound like Spanish, as an attempt to pass themselves off as Cubans. As Cubans, they had a better chance to get games against whites (for some reason, black Cubans were treated better than black Americans at the time), and it also drew better crowds as they sounded more exotic than The Argyle Waiters. Creative team names and player portrayals as exotic or strange were efforts used by black traveling teams into the 1950s.

By the late 1880s there were several black players playing on top semipro, Minor League and

Left: Baseball's first superstar, Adrian "Cap" Anson, drew the color line when he refused to play against black players in the 1880s.

Right: Moses "Fleet" Walker (back row center) was an outstanding catcher for several Organized Baseball teams before the color line was fully instituted.

Major League, and Fleet and his brother Welday were on the team, becoming the first two black players in Major League history, though they were probably forced to the bench several times when facing certain especially bigoted opponents.

In 1885, John W. "Bud" Fowler became the third black player in the Major Leagues when he played for Keokuk in the Western League, then considered a Major League. Fowler and the Walker brothers were the only blacks to play in the Majors until 1947. Fowler, somewhat ironically was born in Cooperstown, New York, near the site of the present day National Baseball Hall of Fame, which has not had a stellar record in inducting deserving black players. Fowler was actually the first black to play on a white professional team, though it was in a Minor League.

In 1886, Fowler was back in Organized Baseball, this time with Topeka in the Western (Minor) League where he hit .300 and played a slick second base. Fleet Walker had moved to Waterbury in the Eastern (Minor) League where he was a good fielding, soft-hitting catcher. Two other blacks came into the Organized Baseball's fold: left-handed George Stovey, the first great pitcher in Black Baseball history with Jersey City of the Eastern League; and Frank Grant, the first true black baseball star, who batted well over .300 with Meridan of the Eastern League and Buffalo of the International (Minor) League. Grant, an all-around star who played anywhere on the diamond, was called the "black Fred Dunlap," after a white player of the time. For the next 60 years black players would often be compared with their white peers: Buck Leonard was the "black Lou Gehrig," Josh Gibson was the "black Babe Ruth," and Jimmie Crutchfield was the "black Lloyd Waner."

It might have appeared in the spring of 1887 that blacks were on their way to making inroads into Organized Baseball as there were about twenty black players on various professional teams. "Fleet" Walker, Fowler, Stovey, and Grant returned and

Major League teams. In 1882, Moses "Fleet" Fleetwood Walker was a catcher with the Toledo Blue Stockings of the Northwestern League, then a Minor League. During that season, Toledo met up against a team led by Hall of Famer Adrian "Cap" Anson, who refused to play if Walker was in the opposing lineup. Organized Baseball, which included Major and Minor League teams, took note and many followed the example set by Anson. In 1883, Toledo entered the American Association, a

were joined by players such as Sol White, a scrappy second baseman with Bellaire of the Ohio State League; Fleet's brother Welday Walker, an outfielder with Akron of the Ohio State League; Richard Johnson, a catcher with Zanesville of the Ohio State League; and Robert Higgins, a pitcher with Syracuse of the International League. Fowler batted over .300, Stovey won thirty games, and Grant was the top all-around hitter in the International League.

It was also in 1887 that Organized Baseball recognized the League of Colored Baseball Clubs as a legitimate Minor League. This league, consisting of teams in Cincinnati, Washington D.C., Louisville, Pittsburgh, Boston, Philadelphia, and New York, would presumably have acted as a feeder league to the Majors. However, the league lasted less than a month; long enough though to show everyone that there were plenty of very good black baseball players, but not yet the fan base to support an entire black league.

It seems strange that 1887 was the year when the color line was ultimately drawn in Organized Baseball. In a game that summer, Anson's Chicago White Stockings were scheduled to play Newark's Eastern League club, who featured black pitcher Stovey. Anson again refused to play an integrated team, and this time his popularity as baseball's first superstar and drawing card proved to be too much for other teams to ignore. Stovey didn't pitch (Newark won anyway) and other white stars followed Anson's lead. Some refused to play against blacks, others refused to even have their photo taken with a black player. There was soon an unwritten rule (it was never written into any league constitutions) in Organized Baseball: No Blacks Allowed. It would be 60 years before this color line was erased.

Using the words "Organized Baseball" is not meant to imply that black teams were unorganized —some were and some were not. It's just a term that was, and has been, accepted to encompass all

Minor and Major League teams. However, some Negro League players did take offense to this term. Connie Johnson, a pitcher with the Kansas City Monarchs, probably the best-run team in segregated baseball once remarked, "We had three sets of uniforms, took the train to our games, had someone take care of our bags, had an All-Star game and a World Series. If that's not organized, I don't know what is."

After the 1887 season, with no other outlet to show off their baseball talents, blacks started forming traveling teams in earnest. They took to the dusty roads of America to play in nearly every one-horse town with a plot of land that could serve as a baseball field.

The first great black team of the "segregated era" was the New York Cuban Giants who were proclaimed (by themselves) black champions in 1887 and 1888. This "original" Cuban Giants team was actually an offshoot of the black waiters from the Argyle Hotel. As was the case with many black teams over the years, the "Argyles," without a scouting or farm system, improved by simply signing the best players from the teams they played. The "Argyles" were originally run by John Lang, a white man, and he immediately signed the best three players from the Philadelphia Orions: George Williams, Abe Harrison, and Shep Trusty. Soon after, the team met a top Philadelphia white team and beat them, then proved their greatness by playing and beating the white Bridgeport, Connecticut team of the Eastern League.

Walter Cook, a white man from Trenton, New Jersey, became the team's backer in 1886 and renamed them the Original Cuban Giants, though the available evidence would suggest that most or all of the players had never been to Cuba, let alone been natives of that country. Cook paid his players according to position; pitchers and catchers received $18 per week plus expenses, infielders got $15, and outfielders $12. The Original Cuban Giants stayed a powerful team through the rest of the 1880s and into the 1890s and were good enough for a *Sporting News* reporter to proclaim them equal to Chicago or New York in the Major Leagues during their heyday. The Original Cuban Giants driving force was second baseman and slugger Frank Grant. Grant, erroneously described

sometimes as a Spaniard because of his light skin, eventually took to wearing wooden shin guards while playing second base as white players tried to spike him while sliding. After his baseball days were over, Grant became a waiter, in a way returning to his baseball roots of the Argyle Hotel.

The next black team to attract significant attention were the New York Gorhams. They won the Eastern Championship in 1887 and 1889 when they played in the Middle States League, an otherwise white semipro league.

To avoid confusion, the word "semipro" should be properly defined. Semipro teams were simply teams that didn't fall under the umbrella of Organized Baseball (Major and Minor League teams) and weren't subject to the rules of a governing body. Semipro teams ranged in talent level from sandlot ball to close to Major League level. These teams were usually sponsored by a large business, factory, shipyard, or municipality and on many of these teams some or all players were paid—pitchers usually making the most money. Semipro leagues, sometimes called "outlaw" baseball, were the only leagues during the 60 years of Organized Baseball segregation where blacks and whites could play against each other, though it was still rare.

The Page Fence Giants were another powerful team of the 1890s, formed in 1894 in Adrian, Michigan, by Bud Fowler and disbanding in 1898. The Page Fence Giants played their home games at Chicago's White Sox Park, and they were recognized as champions in 1895, winning 118 of their 154 games, and again in 1896 after beating the New York Cuban Giants 10 of 15 games.

Page Fence stars included an aging Frank Grant, Sol White, and Grant "Homerun" Johnson, a slugger who studied the art of hitting like Ted Williams would more than a half-century later. The Page Fence Giants traveled in their own train car with their team name painted on the side. The team was also one of the first to inject entertainment into their play to draw bigger crowds. Catching fly balls

Above right: The Page Fence Giants were possibly the first black team to travel in their own train car.

Below right: The Page Fence Giants were one of the first great black teams of the late 1890s.

Right: "Homerun" Johnson studied hitting as a science and starred for many of Black Baseball's early teams..

with one hand during warm-ups (thought to be showboating at the time), and constant chatter during the game kept fans coming back. In the late 1890s, the Page Fence Giants changed their name to the Columbia Giants and had continued success.

Another strong team of the era was the "Genuine" Cuban Giants, not to be confused with the "Original" Cuban Giants. The Cuban X-Giants were the last black powerhouse of the 1800s and the first dynasty in black baseball history, as they were proclaimed champs from 1897 through 1903. The X-Giants, the most traveled team up to that point, were organized by white man E. B. Lamar, Jr. and were captained by Ray Wilson and featured pitchers John Nelson and Dan McClellan, and shortstop "Homerun" Johnson.

As the 1900s opened, there was a changing of the guard in black baseball with the emergence of the Philadelphia Giants as the country's best black team. Many of the same great names were in Giants uniforms: Dan McClellan (who threw a no-hitter in 1903), Frank Grant, and "Homerun" Johnson. New stars included Charlie Grant, who had plied his trade playing with the Page Fence Giants, Columbia Giants, and Cuban X-Giants. Grant was a smooth-fielding second baseman (who eventually replaced Frank Grant as the greatest black player at that position), and was good enough for New York Giants manager John McGraw to try to pass him off as a Native American Indian so he could sign him to a Major League contract. Chicago White Sox owner Charles Comiskey alerted the baseball commissioner's office about the scheme which meant that integration would have to wait.

It should be noted that, although the unwritten rule of Organized Baseball was to exclude blacks, McGraw wasn't the only manager to try to buck this system or sneak around it. In 1916, Jimmy Claxton, a black pitcher, pitched for the Oakland Oaks of the Pacific Coast League, managed by Frank Chance of "Tinkers to Evers to Chance" fame. Claxton pitched both ends of a doubleheader on May 28, but was released on June 3. Other stories abound of white owners trying to convince light-skinned black players to learn Spanish and

pass themselves off as white Cubans in order to enter the Major Leagues, and there was probably a handful who succeeded for periods of time.

By 1905, the Philadelphia Giants were loaded at every position with Pete Hill, one of black baseball's hardest hitters, roaming centerfield from 1903–1907, and right-handed fireballer Andrew "Rube" Foster anchoring the pitching staff. Foster, who gained the nickname "Rube" after beating the Major League pitching star Rube Waddell in

Above: The Cuban X-Giants were the last great black team of the nineteenth century.

Left: Charlie Grant was so good that New York Giants manager John McGraw tried to pass him off as a Cherokee Indian.

1902, reportedly won more than 50 games in 1904 and 1905, some against Major League clubs (although most white teams didn't want blacks on their own teams, they enjoyed the gate receipts from playing against black teams in exhibitions). The Philadelphia Giants beat the Cuban X-Giants to win the championship in 1904, then repeated from 1905 through 1909, winning at least 100 games each year.

In 1905, powerful teams in the Midwest started to form, and the first great team from that area was the Chicago Leland Giants who played at 79th and Wentworth. They were proclaimed Western Champions from 1905–1910, averaging more than 100 wins a year and less than 20 losses. The reason for their success can be traced directly to player-manager Rube Foster, the Roger Clemens of his

players. The 1910 team featured Pete Hill, "Homerun" Johnson, Frank Wickware, Pat Dougherty, and black baseball's newest sensation, John Henry Lloyd—"the Black Honus Wagner." The team won 126 of 134 games, with Foster leading the pitching staff.

In 1911, Foster renamed the team the Chicago American Giants and arranged with a relative of Charles Comiskey's for the team to play at Old White Sox Park on 39th and Wentworth in Chicago. A dynasty was born.

Although Foster, himself, was a large man standing six feet, three inches, the teams he built were known more for their running and bunting, sometimes called "small ball." The American Giants won the Western Championship every year from 1911–1922, except in 1916 when the Indianapolis ABCs temporarily broke their streak.

Foster's teams during this era were led by such players as pitcher "Cannonball" Dick Redding, second baseman Bingo DeMoss, and slugging outfielders Cristobel Torriente and Oscar Charleston.

Foster rarely took the mound for the American Giants, instead concentrating his efforts on becoming the greatest manager in Negro League history and helping make the city of Chicago the Mecca of black baseball for years to come. The Major Leagues' commissioner's office was located in Chicago at the time as well.

During the opening years of the 20th century, the Eastern United States continued to field great teams and one of the strongest was the Brooklyn Royal Giants who won the Eastern Championship in 1909 and 1910.

The New York Lincoln Giants were the next great power of the East, knocking Brooklyn off its perch and winning championships in 1911, 1912, and 1913. They were led by shortstop John Henry Lloyd in his prime, center-fielder Spotswood Poles, catcher Louis Santop, and flame-throwing pitchers Redding and "Smokey" Joe Williams.

Although many teams during the early years of black baseball proclaimed themselves champions, it should be understood that most teams gauged their success on how well they did financially. Unlike the

era, and virtually unbeatable when he was "on." Foster had joined the Lelands after a salary dispute with Philadelphia. During Foster's tenure with the Lelands, blacks on top teams were averaging under $500 per season, compared to $2,000 by Major Leaguers and nearly $600 by Minor Leaguers.

In 1910 Foster "jumped again" when he broke away from Frank Leland and formed his own team made up of former Leland and Philadelphia Giants

Major League teams who strived to win the pennant and World Series, black teams strived for survival—to play another day, meet another payroll, or last another season.

Also, from the very beginning, players moved around to different teams, seemingly indifferent to contracts. Although it may seem that players were money-hungry and disloyal, it should be remembered that there were dozens of teams that lasted mere weeks or days. Players were always looking for a more secure payday. If teams ran into hard times for an extended period of time or incurred some unforeseen expense, it could mean the end of operations. So, when looking at the rosters of teams that survived and flourished during early black baseball history, the same names seem to pop up repeatedly: Pete Hill, Bill Monroe, Frank Grant, "Homerun" Johnson, John Henry Lloyd, Rube Foster, et al.

By the end of the second decade of the 1900s, there were hundreds of outstanding black baseball players, and a lot of revenues being made; big games could draw in excess of 10,000 fans. Baseball, by 1920, was probably the second largest black industry in America behind black-owned insurance companies.

By 1920 black baseball seemed to be at a crossroads. If it were to make the next step toward financial success, full public acceptance, and eventually the integration of Organized Baseball, black baseball needed someone to lead the way. Rube Foster wanted to be that leader and history has shown that he was the right man for the job.

Below left: Standout Ray Beard started catching when masks and shin guards were optional.

Below right: Louis Santop, a top slugger of the dead-ball era, was the favorite catcher of "Cannonball" Dick Redding.

Boom Years

Rube Foster's first Negro National League was formed in 1920 when Foster and several owners of black teams met at the Paseo YMCA in Kansas City. Teams included the Chicago American Giants, Kansas City Monarchs, Chicago Giants, Indianapolis ABCs, St. Louis Giants, Detroit Stars, Dayton Marcos, and Cuban Stars. Foster was the league president (king might have been closer to the truth) and he set the rules: players were to conduct themselves professionally on and off the field; if one team was weak he reserved the right to shift players around or lend teams money to keep the entire league strong and competitive. Foster, a "big picture" thinker, even gave his best player, Oscar Charleston, to the Indianapolis ABCs to give the league more parity.

It was not Foster's vision to be a farm system to the Majors, but, instead, to get to a point where entire Negro League teams would enter the Major League ranks.

In 1920, the Chicago American Giants won the league pennant with a 32-13 record. They repeated this in 1921 and 1922 with records of 42-22 and 36-23, respectively. Kansas City won in 1923, 1924, and 1925.

Starting in 1924, Foster instituted a split-season schedule with each half's winner playing a flag series at the end of the season. This format, and the extra games and excitement it created, put some extra money into the league's coffers, though not as much as Foster might have envisioned.

Below: This team, sponsored by the Chicago, Milwaukee and St. Paul Railroad, was one of the top black traveling teams of the 1920s.

Right: William "Bobby" Robinson, an acrobatic third baseman, broke in with the Indianapolis ABCs in the 1925.

Below: Rube Foster (second from left) and C.I. Taylor (far right) were the premier managers of the early Negro National League.

Not all was peaches and cream for the Negro National League in the beginning (or ever, for that matter) and despite Foster's attempt for league parity, some teams came and went quickly, usually due to a lack of fan interest. The Columbus Buckeyes joined the Negro National League and folded in 1921, followed by the Pittsburgh Keystones (1922), Cleveland Tate Stars (1922), Milwaukee Bears (1923), Toledo Tigers (1923), and Cleveland Browns (1924). Teams suffered and teams died, but the league survived.

In 1923, the Eastern Colored League was formed among the top Eastern teams, including the Atlantic City Bacharachs, Philadelphia Hilldales, New York Lincoln Giants, Baltimore Black Sox, Brooklyn Royal Giants, and the "Eastern" Cuban Stars.

As might be expected with competition, Eastern teams started "raiding" Negro National

Above: Ted "Double Duty" Radcliffe was a top pitcher and catcher in the Negro Leagues for more than 30 years.

Right: Sam Bankhead, one of five brothers to play in the Negro Leagues, played every position on the diamond.

League rosters, offering more money to the best players and some of them jumped their contracts. When the Harrisburg Giants lured Oscar Charleston from the ABCs, Foster went through the roof. The league he had created was starting to show cracks. But Foster turned the competition into a positive, and in 1924 the Negro National League and Eastern League would face off in the first Negro League World Series.

The Negro League World Series was an attempt to bring more prestige to the Negro Leagues, to fill the coffers at the end of the season, and to try to show white society that the black leagues were just like the Big Leagues. Unfortunately, the Negro League's version of the Fall Classic never did catch the black public's fancy and for many seasons wasn't played at all.

Because Negro League teams first and foremost wanted to survive, the team that won the pennant or championship wasn't always of top importance. The Negro National League tried to have a balanced schedule, with most teams traveling by train. But uncontrollable variables such as bad weather, travel problems, and teams jumping at offers to play non-league games for guaranteed money made this difficult.

In one of the Negro National League's first seasons, for example, the Chicago American Giants played 62 games against other Negro National League teams. The Kansas City Monarchs played 81; St. Louis Giants, 56; Detroit Stars, 57; Indianapolis ABCs, 59; Columbus Buckeyes, 72; Cuban Stars, 62; and Chicago Giants, 42. Because of this, league champions, as well as league leaders in batting average, homers, pitching wins, and strikeouts were always hard to nail down. Knowledgeable fans often argued that the teams in the Negro League World Series were not, in fact, the best teams.

In reality, the big money to be made after the regular season was not in the Negro League World Series, but in exhibitions between black All-Star teams and white Big Leaguers. Black and white teams often played 10–20 games in the fall and it was probable that black players could make more in a few weeks playing exhibitions against Major Leaguers than in an entire season in the Negro

Leagues. As a result, sometimes Negro Leaguers were disappointed to play in the Negro World Series simply because they could make more money elsewhere!

The biggest blow to the Negro Leagues reputation and success came in December of 1930 when Rube Foster passed away after spending the last few years of his life in a mental hospital. The Negro National League had been Foster's vision and he was the unchallenged captain of the operation. Foster's death left a void that was never filled. That's not to say that teams and players weren't successful and first rate, but the leagues in which Negro League teams played were never run with the same professionalism as when Foster was at the helm.

Most Negro Leaguers had instances in which their teams couldn't pay them on time or at all, many team owners were involved in organized crime, and there were other undesirables that were necessary evils to many teams. Nat Strong, for example, was a monopolistic booking agent for teams in the East, and if teams wanted to play in certain stadiums (Yankee Stadium, the Polo Grounds, Dexter Park) they had to go through him, and give him a cut of the gate receipts. In the West, Abe Saperstein, an honest man according to Negro League players, was nonetheless a necessary conduit to get into certain stadiums. Some stadium owners would rent their fields to a white man like Saperstein but not to a black man.

Double Duty Radcliffe, a player and manager for more than 30 years, believed the players in the Negro Leagues to be of Major League quality, but insisted that the Negro Leagues were sometimes run "like a semipro booking agency." Many players played without contracts, and contracts that were signed weren't enforced.

The average Negro Leaguer probably played with at least a handful of teams, "jumping" often for more money. The only teams that seemed to keep the same players from year to year consistently were the Homestead Grays and Kansas City Monarchs, two teams that were well-run and almost never missed a payday.

A Negro Leaguer's life was very similar to that of a white player in Class C or Class D ball. The salaries were similar, with the average player making from $150 to $400 a month, plus about 50¢ a day meal money, and the travel was never-ending. The only major difference was the segregation the Negro Leaguers had to deal with. Where white players could eat and sleep anywhere they wanted (assuming they could afford it), Negro Leaguers often existed on a diet of peanut butter sandwiches and sardines, and had to be able to sleep anywhere at anytime, including dugouts, tents, buses, or standing up.

Negro League teams carried as few as 12 men some years and in the 1930s and 1940s gave up train travel for buses or cars. Because a Negro League team's roster didn't carry many extra players, everyone was expected to be versatile. Pitchers needed to be able to hit and play outfield if needed, and anyone with a strong arm was expected to be able to pitch if called upon.

This is why many Negro Leaguers believed that the quality of play in the Negro Leagues was usually Triple-A Minor League caliber. Where the Major Leagues had good backups at every position and 8 to 10 fine pitchers, some Negro League teams had only a few good pitchers and often had players playing out of position when a player went down with injuries.

The Major Leagues had sophisticated scouting systems with which they found and developed talent. Negro League teams, in turn, had no formal scouting at all. They sometimes got tips from black college coaches touting certain players, but most Negro League teams discovered players by playing against them. For instance, if the Memphis Red Sox were playing the Blue City Blues (an actual team) and one of the Blues, "Black Bottom" Bluford (an actual player!) had a great game, the Red Sox manager would approach him after the game.

"Mr. Buford, how much money do you make on the Blues?" the manager might ask.

"I make $100 a month," might come the answer.

"We'll give you $125 a month to come with us," the manager might counter. Nine times out of 10 the player would "jump" to the higher paying team.

It's all the more incredible that the Negro Leagues were able to produce so many outstanding players. Although teams like the Chicago American Giants or Birmingham Black Barons might have been Triple-A caliber, when the Negro Leagues put together All-Star teams with the best players from various teams, they simply overmatched their Major League counterparts.

In the hundreds of games played between Negro League and Major League All-Star squads, the Negro Leaguers won about 60 percent of the time. Most of the time, these games were played at the pace of normal Major League schedules—that is to say, there were usually single games, played on manicured Major League or Minor League fields, with batting and fielding practice beforehand. In other words, the opposite of what Negro Leaguers were used to.

Rarely during the regular season did Negro Leaguers have time to leisurely prepare for a game. They usually came into a town, played a game, and quickly crammed back into a pair of cars, sweaty and tired, and went to a town hundreds of miles away to play another game or two!

It's no wonder, then, that Negro Leaguers dominated in these black-white match-ups. Compared to their normal games, these exhibitions were like vacations. "Double Duty" Radcliffe, for example, played 36 years in the Negro Leagues and batted .303 in more than 10,000 at bats, but against Major Leaguers he batted over .400 and also pitched several games without a defeat.

It usually surprises baseball fans to learn that the majority of games that black teams played in the 1920s, 1930s, and 1940s were against white semi-pro teams—surprising since the only reason there were black teams at all was because blacks were shunned by white professional leagues. But during the early 1900s virtually every town, factory, shipyard, and post office had a semipro team, and games against these teams were the bread and butter for most black teams.

Some factory teams, such as the Denver Fuels, were sponsored by million-dollar companies, had

Right: Maceo Breedlove (left) was a pitcher who was moved to the outfield to get his bat in the lineup everyday, a la Babe Ruth.

Above: The 1925 Bertha (Minnesota) Fishermen fielded one of the country's few integrated semipro teams when it hired John Donaldson (middle row, third from left) to pitch every big game.

air-conditioned buses, and hired ex-Major and Minor Leaguers. Some towns, such as Fairmont, Minnesota, might have a farmer on first base and a butcher in right field. Make no mistake, though, fans came out in droves to watch the black-white match-ups.

As a general rule, Negro League teams destroyed white semipro teams, and the semipro teams knew the probable outcome when they scheduled the game. But in small towns across the country, it was not only a chance to see how the locals stacked up against Major League-caliber teams, but it was also a chance to see black people in person. A Jamestown, North Dakota, baseball fan recalled being encouraged by his mother to "go see how they talk" when the Kansas City Monarchs came to town.

Since Negro League teams usually over-matched their white counterparts anyway and because they wanted to be invited back, they usually tried not to embarrass their opposition, usually calling off the dogs once they had a comfortable lead.

Negro Leaguer Norman Lumpkin explained that acting, besides pitching and hitting, was a skill that black players had to have. "We were good actors," said Lumpkin. "You had to be a good actor to survive. We learned the hard way, because if you'd run the score up and act like you enjoyed beating 'em, those people really did run your ass out of town. It's a fact."

There were a few semipro teams too that were integrated. Teams such as Little Falls, Crookston, and Bertha, Minnesota, hired black pitchers such as John Donaldson, Webster McDonald, and Chet Brewer to be their "featured pitcher"—meaning they would pitch almost every game.

Bertha, a town of under 1,000, once drew almost 10,000 fans to a game when Donaldson pitched against a town rival. Semipro teams were sometimes called "outlaw" teams because they didn't have to answer to anyone and sometimes hired blacks and other players shunned from Organized Baseball.

During the depression, some of the better Negro League teams such as the Homestead Grays, Pittsburgh Crawfords, Kansas City Monarchs, and Chicago American Giants, dropped out of the Negro Leagues and simply barnstormed from Memorial Day through Labor Day. They still played against Negro League teams, but weren't mandated by any league officials on when and who to play.

Two of Negro League history's greatest teams, the 1931 Grays (136 wins, 17 losses) and 1932 Pittsburgh Crawfords (99-36), weren't in any league but instead played black and white teams all over the eastern part of the country and then proclaimed themselves champions.

Teams such as the Gilkerson Union Giants, Illinois Giants, Detroit Acme Giants, and Harlem Globetrotters were never in an organized league, but just barnstormed in a chosen area of the United States from April through September.

Above: The 1931 Crookston, Minnesota team never lost a game once they hired pitcher Chet Brewer (top row, third from right).

Left: In 1931, Webster McDonald turned Little Falls, Minnesota into Baseball City, USA by beating the Minor's Minneapolis Millers.

Above: John Donaldson (back row, third from left) played for several Midwest towns for more money than the Negro Leagues offered.

Besides the Negro National League and Eastern Colored League, which were quite successful, all things considered, there were many leagues that came and went in a hurry. The American Negro League (1929–1931) and East-West League (1932) folded quickly, while the Negro Southern League reinvented itself many times, fielding teams many of the years of the 1930s and 1940s. There were also leagues considered black Minor Leagues such as the Texas Negro League, Arkansas Negro League, West Coast Negro League, and Negro American Association.

If you were a talented black baseball player in the early part of the 20th century, you could probably make a decent living playing baseball, but there were no long-term contracts (unless you think a month is long term), no pension, and if you got injured you probably wouldn't get paid at all.

Despite all the negatives, Negro League players wouldn't have missed their ballplaying days for the world. "I just loved it," remembered Lester Lockett, a slugging outfielder. "Kind of think I'd like to go back and do it again. But I better get another body, hadn't I?"

The fact is, for a black man, a baseball career was one of the few opportunities available to make a good living. Most Negro Leaguers made several times in salary what their fathers had, and Negro Leaguers were celebrities in their communities.

The Negro National League shut down during the heart of the depression, then reinvented itself in 1933 and included many of the towns from the old Eastern Colored League: Pittsburgh Crawfords, New York Cubans, Homestead Grays, Brooklyn Eagles (became Newark Eagles), Columbus Elite Giants (later Washington, Baltimore, and Nashville), Philadelphia Stars, Newark Dodgers, and Cole's American Giants of Chicago. Most of these teams would survive into the late 1940s.

The Negro American League formed in 1937, and included teams in cities most associated with the original Negro National League: the Kansas City Monarchs, Chicago American Giants, Memphis Red Sox, Atlanta Black Crackers, Birmingham Black Barons, Indianapolis ABCs, and Jacksonville Red Sox. Most of these teams would also survive for more than a decade.

The Negro Southern League was looked at as a Minor League because its teams weren't covered by the two leading black newspapers of the time, the *Chicago Defender* and the *Pittsburgh Courier*. They included, at one time or another, teams including the Atlanta Black Crackers, Monroe Monarchs, Chattanooga Black Lookouts, Chattanooga Choo Choos, Mobile Black Bears, Montgomery Gray Sox, Houston Black Buffaloes,

Above: Future Negro League stars "Double Duty" Radcliffe (front row, second from left) and Red Haley (front row, far right) started with traveling teams like the Illinois Giants.

Asheville Blues, New Orleans Black Pelicans, Little Rock Black Travelers, and Knoxville Grays. Players such as Hilton Smith, Turkey Stearnes, and Willie Mays came out of this league and went on to the Hall of Fame.

The 1930s saw many innovations that helped keep the Negro Leagues alive. Lighted fields and night games kept many Negro League teams viable during the depression, because most adults had to work and couldn't attend games during the day.

During the 1930s, there were a few fields with lights—Greenlee Field in Pittsburgh and Osbourne Stadium in Winnipeg, Manitoba, in Canada—but the Kansas City Monarchs solved the problem by carrying their own lights with them. The Monarchs would pull up to a ball park, unload several light standards off flat bed trucks, then hook them into a generator in the outfield. The lights didn't stand high enough to be very effective and were not very powerful, but fans came out to see the entire production, from setup to the game. These lights also led to some great pitching duels, and opponents often begged the Monarchs pitchers, especially "Satchel" Paige, to take it easy. "One guy said, 'It's a shame to throw Paige under these lights, when you can't see him during the day!' " remembered "Double Duty" Radcliffe.

The other great innovation of the 1930s was the East-West All-Star game, the crown jewel of black baseball. In 1933, the same year the Major

Leagues held their first All-Star game, Crawfords' owner Gus Greenlee and Harlem Globetrotter owner Abe Saperstein conceived of and promoted a game which would feature the best players from the top Negro League teams, by vote of the fan, and it soon became the biggest game of the year— much bigger than the Negro League World Series. Unlike the Major League All-Star game, which rotated to a different ball park each year, the East-West game was played at Comiskey Park in Chicago every year from 1933 until 1960.

Several years the East-West games outdrew the Major League All-Star game, and crowds close to 50,000 were not unusual. Teams in the league shared the game's revenues, and because it was played late in the season, it sometimes wiped out the debts of many teams and kept them alive to play another season.

Players made a little extra money, usually around $25 plus expenses, but the memories and prestige of playing in these games were worth more than money to some players.

Outfielder Jimmie Crutchfield, claimed the thrill of playing in the East-West game was worth more than a million dollars and "Double Duty"

Radcliffe, who played for 36 years and was on several championship teams, called a home run he hit in the 1944 East-West game his greatest thrill.

The East-West game was great and night games were a novelty, but the Negro Leagues might never have had any so-called "boom years" if not for the greatest showman in baseball history—Leroy "Satchel" Paige.

It's no coincidence that the boom years of the Negro Leagues virtually mirrored the career of Paige. There was never a bigger drawing card, before or since, and Paige, as much as any innovation or All-Star game, kept the Negro Leagues alive and profitable.

Paige was born in Mobile, Alabama, around the turn of the century, and entered the black big leagues in the late 1920s with the Birmingham Black Barons. By 1932, Paige was the greatest pitcher on earth as a member of the Pittsburgh Crawfords, and over the next 20 years, whenever a team needed financial help, they called for Satchel, who would pitch for anyone, anywhere, for the right price.

Paige's demands were usually a guarantee up-front (anywhere from $100–$1,000), plus a cut of the gate, and a decent place to sleep and eat. If towns wanted Paige to pitch, but wouldn't let him eat or sleep at their restaurants or hotels, Paige wouldn't come. Paige knew his personality and

skinny right arm were a valuable commodity and he refused second-class treatment.

Semipro teams or Negro League teams would often base their year's budget on an appearance by Paige, and the pitcher kept many teams in the depression from going bankrupt by pitching a single game.

Not only was Paige virtually unhittable in his prime, but he had the uncanny ability to pitch almost everyday. It may sound like pure legend, but there truly were dozens of times that Paige called in his fielders for the last innings of games, knowing that no one on earth could hit his tremendous fastball. While Paige's fielders sat behind the mound playing cards, Paige would strikeout the side to the delight of screaming fans.

Dr. Bob Price, a semipro player from Texas, recalled his meeting with Paige more than a half-century ago: "The umpire called me out and I never heard such an ovation for striking out. We got beat but nobody expected us to win anyway. I remember riding home in the truck with my Dad and him saying, 'Son, I'm proud of you. You were struck out by the great Satchel Paige!'"

Out of the Negro Leagues boom years came some of the greatest players in baseball history, and games that will be forever part of Negro League lore.

Left: Alec Radcliffe, brother of "Double Duty" Radcliffe, was the hardest-hitting third baseman of the 1930s.

Right: The Twin Cities Colored Giants once had to pawn some watches to buy gas to get to their next game.

Integration

Right: Bill "Ready" Cash could hit, catch and throw, but he wasn't allowed to do so in the Major Leagues.

Far right: In the 1940s Bob Feller barnstormed against black players, but didn't believe they were Major League material.

It could be argued that the seeds of integration were planted the very day Organized Baseball became segregated in the 1880s. Every so often a sportswriter, after watching his local team get beat, would lament in print, "wouldn't some great black players make our club better?" Others, after watching blacks compete, and dominate, in track, boxing, and other sports, would ask "why not in baseball?"

For years Organized Baseball's official opinion on integration was that they had no opinion. "They have their league and we have ours," owners would state. "Everyone seems to be happy."

Some owners, when pressed, would cling to the theory that blacks weren't good enough to play in the Majors, and baseball commissioner Judge Landis tried to keep this theory alive by banning intact Major League teams from playing against Negro League teams. In other words, the St. Louis Cardinals couldn't play the Kansas City Monarchs, but the Dizzy Dean All-Stars (basically the St. Louis Cardinals with some other players added) could play the Satchel Paige All-Stars. That way, no one could claim that a Negro League team beat a Major League team. After all, the Dizzy Dean All-Stars don't try their hardest when playing Negro Leaguers in the off-season, right? The argument might have held water if the games between Negro Leaguers and Major League All-Star teams had been evenly split, but, the fact is, the Negro Leaguers won about 60 percent of the time. Dizzy Dean, a Southerner with a great appreciation for baseball talent, black or white, proclaimed "Satchel" Paige the best pitcher he ever saw, and reaped praise on many other Negro Leaguers.

As a general rule, Major Leaguers who barnstormed against Negro Leaguers spoke glowingly of their black counterparts' talents. Lou Gehrig, Joe DiMaggio, Ted Williams, Rudy York, and other Major League stars complimented the play of Negro Leaguers and publicly stated that they would welcome them into the Majors.

There are several reasons for this feeling among the elite players: firstly, great players usually love to be challenged and they knew that if the

Left: Bubba Hyde played integrated baseball in three countries but the United States wasn't one of them.

Right: The Minor League's Oakland Oaks signed several black players in the 1940s and 1950s including Alonzo Perry (third from left) and Artie Wilson (far right).

```
```

```
```

best Negro Leaguers were added to the Majors, it would only improve the entire league. Secondly, players like Joe DiMaggio and Ted Williams knew that no Negro League player would ever take their job. It was the lesser players, the 24th or 25th man on a big league roster who really had something to worry about and these fringe players shuddered at the prospect of integration. For them it could mean being sent to a life of hard labor in a coal mine or factory.

Above: Judge Landis may have saved baseball after the "Black Sox" scandal, but he fought against integration.

In the United States, many wondered, "if black sportsmen can dominate in track and boxing, why not baseball." More importantly, why not at least give them a chance to try?

There were teams that did give black players a chance, but these were all semipro teams, and did not fall under the umbrella of Organized Baseball and its regulations. Towns in Minnesota such as Bertha, Little Falls, Crookston, and Winona, and North Dakota towns such as Bismarck, Jamestown, New Rockford, and Valley City hired black players to bolster their teams, and some became as powerful as any team in any league.

The 1935 Bismarck Churchills featured a pitching staff of "Satchel" Paige, Barney Morris, Hilton Smith, "Double Duty" Radcliffe, and Chet Brewer, as well as Negro League stars Quincy Trouppe, Red Haley, and Art Hancock, and white stars Moose Johnson, Ed Hendee, Axel Leary, Bob McCarney, Dan Oberholzer, and Joe Desiderato. The team's owner, Neil O. Churchill, gave the baseball world a glimpse of what integration could be more than a decade before Branch Rickey. Churchill, with the help of Harlem Globetrotter's owner Abe Saperstein, hired the greatest players available, black or white, and the team was one of the best of its time. Bismarck played to packed houses at home, and traveled around the Midwest, destroying its competition. It crowned the season by winning the first National Semipro Tournament in Wichita, Kansas, in seven straight games against teams loaded with Major and Minor Leaguers.

In 1936, Major League legend Honus Wagner was named commissioner of the National Semipro Tournament on a board with Ty Cobb and Walter Johnson. One of Wagner's first acts as commissioner was to outlaw "mixed" (integrated) teams in the national tournament, although he did allow Bismarck to defend its title. Bismarck, though, without Paige, who had jumped to the Kansas City Monarchs, were knocked out of the tournament despite four wins by Hilton Smith.

One of the first significant events to bring the issue of race to the front page of newspapers was the 1936 Olympics in Berlin, Germany. Adolf Hitler was among 100,000 in Berlin's Olympic Stadium, when Jesse Owens destroyed the Nazi's theory of the "superior Aryan race" by winning four gold medals and setting seven Olympic records. It's somewhat ironic, too, that Owens won the 200 meter dash by edging out Mack Robinson, Jackie Robinson's brother. Hitler, looking and acting the fool, refused to present medals to Owens.

Another significant event was the rise of boxer Joe Louis to the heavyweight championship of the world. Louis won the crown in 1937 by beating James J. Braddock in Comiskey Park. It was said that the boxing ring was the only place a black man could beat a white man without repercussions. Louis' victory in 1938 against German Max Schmeling in 124 seconds made Louis the most famous black athlete in the world, as it was billed as the "Aryan master-race versus the freed slave."

Above right: Here a Midwest town of 300 drew more than 5,000 fans to see John Donaldson pitch for an integrated club.

Below right: Dave Brown (back row, third from right) left the Negro Leagues after a brush with the law, and played integrated semipro ball in the Midwest for years.

Above: The 1932 Pittsburgh Crawfords featuring "Satchel" Paige (back row, second from left) and Josh Gibson (to Paige's left) "played like they invented the game."

In 1938, Lloyd Lewis, the white sports editor of the *Chicago Daily News*, attended the East-West game at Comiskey Park and came away utterly impressed. He proclaimed Negro Leaguers lacking in textbook batting form, but more daring in their baserunning and fielding. Lewis thought Willie Wells was better than most Major League short-stops and, after watching Hilton Smith, "Double Duty" Radcliffe, Barney Brown, and "Schoolboy" Johnny Taylor, thought that Negro Leaguers could fill pitching slots on the leading teams in the Big Leagues.

In 1942, Brooklyn Dodger manager Leo Durocher, his team in the middle of a season in which they would finish second to the St. Louis Cardinals, mentioned to a reporter that if the commissioner's office would let him sign black players, he could win the pennant. Landis responded by stating that there was no rule in Organized Baseball banning blacks. The unwritten rule of segregation had been around for so many years, that this statement caught many off guard. "You mean the

Washington Senators could hire Josh Gibson and Buck Leonard if they wanted?" thought some fans.

"The question of Negroes in the Majors," wrote Atlanta columnist Luscious Jones, "has never been one of ability. It's purely a matter of color." Jones was correct, though it wasn't simply a matter of skin color. It was also about the color green, as in money. Major and Minor League teams made a lot of money by renting their ball parks to Negro League teams. In the history of the Negro Leagues, only the Pittsburgh Crawfords, with its own Greenlee Field, played rent free. Teams such as the New York Black Yankees (Yankee Stadium), New York Cubans (Polo Grounds), Homestead Grays (Forbes Field and Griffith Stadium) and Memphis Red Sox (Martin Park) paid rent to play in Major and Minor League parks—though they usually weren't allowed to use the showers. The New York Yankees probably made more than $100,000 a year from rent to Negro Leaguers.

Above right: The integrated 1935 Bismarck Churchills won the first National Semipro Tournament led by "Satchel Paige" (back row, center), "Double Duty "Radcliffe (back row, far right), Quincy Trouppe (next to Radcliffe) and Hilton Smith (back row, far left).

Below right: Teams like the Broadway Clowns mixed baseball with entertainment, sometimes performing skits between innings.

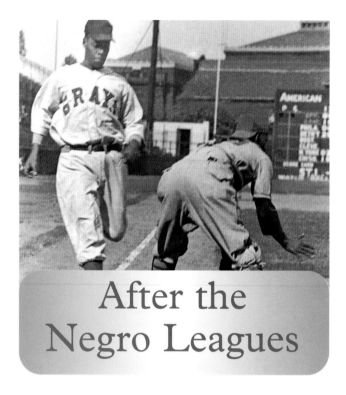

After the Negro Leagues

Starting in the early 1940s, black players were watched carefully by Major and Minor League scouts, knowing that segregation wouldn't last forever. There were also many newspaper reporters, black and white, wondering aloud when certain teams would use their brains and sign some black talent.

In 1943, the Los Angeles Angels of the Pacific Coast League offered tryouts to Chet Brewer, Howard Easterling, and Nate Moreland, then rescinded at the last minute. The Oakland Oaks, also of the Pacific Coast League, considered a tryout for Brewer, but the team's manager refused.

In 1943, Bill Veeck, one of the greatest baseball minds of any era, hatched an idea which, if allowed to proceed, would have changed baseball history forever. The Philadelphia Phillies, the doormat of the National League for years, were for sale and Veeck devised a plan where he would buy the team and fill its roster with players from the Negro Leagues. Veeck's idea was leaked to Commissioner Landis and the Phillies were quickly sold to another buyer.

1944 was a turning point in the road to integration because of two significant events: the height of World War II and the death of Major League commissioner Landis. The fact that black men were dying on foreign battlefields in the name of freedom, made blacks and whites at home wonder why the national pastime would shut them out. Then, when Landis died, many owners saw the event as a green light to scout Negro Leaguers because it became obvious the time for integration was drawing near.

The man who replaced Landis as baseball commissioner was former Kentucky Governor, senator Albert "Happy" Chandler. In the spring of 1945, Chandler said he would "consider the black question." "This is a free country and everybody should have an equal opportunity," he said. "I know nothing, from fact, of any discrimination against Negroes in the Big Leagues. There is no rule against them. On the other hand, nobody can guarantee that they make the grade. That's a matter of their own ability." Many black fans were nervous at Chandler's remarks that there was no discrimination in the Big Leagues. Nerves were tested further when Chandler bragged about how he solved segregation at the University of Kentucky by "establishing a first class college for colored folks."

Eventually, Chandler went against the "good ol' boy network" in baseball by backing baseball integration. His reasoning? He explained later in life that he didn't want to meet his maker one day having made the wrong decision on such an important issue.

In 1945, pitcher Terris McDuffie and first baseman "Showboat" Thomas were given tryouts with the Brooklyn Dodgers as a response to public pressure. Team president Branch Rickey, who had his own plan in the works, attended the tryout and said neither were Big League material. In fairness, both players were past their prime; McDuffie still had great control but his speed was gone, and Thomas, who never had been a great hitter, was known as a showboating fielder, something not seen in the Majors.

That same year the Boston Red Sox and Boston Braves refused to give black players tryouts, and it turned out to be a public relations nightmare. First, black sportwriter Wendell Smith attacked the Boston teams in the press, and Boston city councilman Isadore Muchnick threatened to withhold Sunday baseball permits unless black players were at least given a tryout.

So under great pressure, the Red Sox gave try-outs to Jackie Robinson, Sam Jethroe, and Marvin Williams. All three players had impressive tryouts, but nothing came of it (though Robinson and Jethroe would both have great Major League careers, and Williams would have a great Minor League career).

Branch Rickey had become president of the Brooklyn Dodgers in 1942 and began a plan to integrate Organized Baseball. In 1945, he sent his top scout, Clyde Sukeforth, on a search for the right candidate to integrate baseball. Rickey, through the years, has become a romantic figure and is erroneously remembered by some as a man with only the betterment of mankind at heart.

The fact is, Rickey was a very religious man who felt deeply that integration was the right thing

Left: Artie Wilson was considered by many to be a "can't miss" Major League prospect, but he spent most of his post-Negro League career in the Minors.

Below: Quincy Trouppe (seated, far left) had a cup of coffee in the Majors when he was well past his prime.

to do, but he was also a smart businessman who sought out a plan to make integration as profitable as possible.

Rickey's key concern in signing Negro Leaguers was the cost to buy their contracts. As a frame of reference, at one time a Major League team might pay a Minor League team $25,000–$100,000 for the contract of a top prospect such as Lefty Grove or Ted Williams. When Rickey was the general manager of the St. Louis Cardinals in the 1920s and 30s, he tried to change this system by developing the "farm system" where Major League teams would own Minor League teams and, thus, wouldn't have to go out and bid with Major League teams for Minor League stars—the Minor Leaguers in their farm systems were their property. After the Cardinals fielded powerful teams year after year, the rest of the Major League's teams adopted this method of developing players.

With regards to signing Negro Leaguers, Rickey was faced with the prospect of returning to the "old system" of scouting and bidding for players. Since, for instance, the Homestead Grays weren't owned by a Major League team, theoretically, Major League teams would have to bid for players such as Buck Leonard, Josh Gibson, and Raymond Brown, and pay big money to the Grays for their contracts. Rickey thought there was a better, cheaper way to get Negro League players.

Rickey first announced publicly that he thought the Negro Leagues were not legitimate leagues, but were more akin to a racket because many of the league's owners were racketeers (which they were). Rickey's disparaging remarks were his way of discrediting the Negro Leagues and, therefore, would allow him to sign its players without compensation, as was the normal protocol when dealing with a Minor League team.

Next, Rickey formed a black league called the United States League featuring the Pittsburgh Crawfords, Detroit Motor City Giants, Toledo Rays, Philadelphia Hilldale Giants, and his own Brooklyn Brown Dodgers, managed by Oscar Charleston. Oddly, Rickey gave the Crawfords franchise to Gus Greenlee, the Negro League's racketeer extraordinaire and "numbers king" of Pittsburgh's black community.

Rickey's league, supposedly, was a "more legitimate" place for black players. In reality, with the new league, Rickey could now evaluate black players out in the open, without competition from other Big League teams and could send scouts to Negro League games under the guise of looking for players for his new league. Of course, his scouts were really looking for players for the Major League Dodgers, not the "Brown Dodgers." Sounds complicated? It was.

The United States League performed about as well as can be expected, and as well as it needed to. The league played most of its games on schedule, and attracted some decent players. During the season, Dodger scout Sukeforth followed the Kansas City Monarchs, supposedly as a scout for the Brown Dodgers, and became interested in rookie Jackie Robinson. Robinson was playing out of position at shortstop due to an injury to regular Jesse Williams, and he had trouble making the long throw from the hole. But the fire Robinson played with made everyone notice him.

In Robinson, Sukeforth saw a sensational athlete, with a background of integrated college athletics, and a desire and drive to succeed that could not be taught.

As the Negro League season was winding down, Robinson was summoned to a meeting with Rickey, where Robinson thought he would be offered a contract with the Brown Dodgers. Of course Rickey's offer was for the Major League Dodgers, and the color line, at long last, was wiped away.

Robinson, when interviewed, seemed humbled by the enormity of the situation, but firmly stated that he would "do [his] very best to come through in every manner" for he knew how much it meant to baseball and his race.

On the financial side, the Kansas City Monarchs didn't receive any compensation for Robinson and they were angry. The Monarchs management knew, however, that a lawsuit would be suicide, because who would want to stand in the way of baseball integration?

Banner headlines screamed the news of Jackie Robinson, best known as UCLA's hotshot

Above: Pitcher Roy Partlow replaced Johnny Wright as Jackie Robinson's roommate on the 1946 Montreal Royals.

A scout for the Boston Red Sox, the last team to integrate, said he thought it was the worst thing that could happen to Organized Baseball. Many Big Leaguers said they didn't care as long as Robinson wasn't on their team, and Hall of Famer Rogers Hornsby said simply: "they should stay in their own league." There were a few brave souls like Detroit Tiger star Rudy York who publicly wished Robinson luck, but most Major Leaguers, it seemed, held their breath.

In 1946, the Dodgers assigned Robinson to their top Minor League team, the Montreal Royals of the International League. Robinson quickly proved all his critics wrong, and eased the minds of many of his supporters when he went four for five with a homer, two stolen bases, and four runs in his first game for Montreal.

Joining Robinson on the Royals was Johnny Wright, a pitcher from the Homestead Grays, who seemed overwhelmed and was optioned to a lower level team in the Dodger farm system. Later in the season, Roy Partlow, another pitcher from the Grays played briefly with Robinson, but also was farmed out. In hindsight, it looks like Wright and Partlow were used more as roommates for the solitary Robinson, rather than as legitimate Big League prospects, because both pitchers, though great in their prime, were already 29 and 34 years old, respectively, by this stage.

Robinson, thus, would spend most of the season as a solitary black figure in an otherwise lily white league. Although the pressure was incredible and the stakes enormous, Robinson would finish as the league's best player with a .349 average, 40 stolen bases, and a .985 fielding percentage at second base—all league-leading figures. More importantly and consistent with Robinson's drive to win, he led Montreal to the International League pennant, and the "Little World Series" championship over the American Association's Louisville Red Birds.

After the 1946 season, Robinson formed an All-Star team that barnstormed on the West Coast against Major Leaguers. Robinson's team featured Monte Irvin, Larry Doby, and white player Al Campanis. Campanis, a teammate and great friend to Robinson on the Montreal Royals, is best known as a successful Dodgers general manager in the

half-back, being signed by the Dodgers. The news drew immediate and varied reactions. Negro Leaguers such as "Satchel" Paige and Josh Gibson were somewhat bitter that they, instead, weren't chosen. Most other Negro Leaguers were worried. Worried because integration would soon mean the death of the Negro Leagues and hundreds of jobs, and worried because Robinson wasn't, in their eyes, a "can't miss prospect."

"If Jackie doesn't do well, how long will we have to wait to get another chance?" was a thought often expressed by Negro Leaguers. Below the Mason-Dixon Line, the news went over like a lead balloon. "We live happier with segregation," wrote one newspaper editor.

Right: Roy Partlow was given the chance to become the first black pitcher in the modern Major Leagues, but he struggled with Montreal.

1970s and 1980s who was fired after a television interview in 1987 in which he said black players lacked the "necessities" to be managers and executives in the Majors.

Robinson's team faced an All-Star team led by pitching great Bob Feller, and Robinson belted two doubles off the Major League ace.

"Satchel" Paige also had an All-Star team on the Coast, and they, too, gave Feller's team fits. "Bob Feller had his butt kicked royally against black teams on the barnstorming tours," remembered Negro Leaguer Maurice Peatros. "He got hit so hard, man, and the people were booing. He did not believe anybody could hit his fastball!"

What is interesting isn't that Negro Leaguers had some success against a great pitcher like Feller. What is interesting is that Feller didn't seem to want to acknowledge the skills of the black players.

As Feller was leaving the clubhouse after one game that fall, a *Sporting News* reporter questioned him on the qualifications of Negro Leaguers. "Do you think they'll make the Big League grade?" asked the reporter. "Haven't seen one—not one," fired back Feller. "Maybe [Satchel] Paige when he was young. When you name him you're done. Some are good hitters, some can field pretty good, most of them are fast. But I have seen none who combines the qualities of a Big League player."

"Not even Jackie Robinson?" pressed the reporter.

"Not even Jackie Robinson," answered Feller.

Well, a great pitcher Feller was, but a scout he was not. Robinson opened the 1947 season with the Brooklyn Dodgers and continued his excellent play. After a slow start, Robinson, playing first base for the first time in his career, led the Dodgers to their first pennant since 1941, and only their fifth pennant in the 20th century. Robinson led the Dodgers in runs, hits, doubles (tied), homers (tied), slugging, and stolen bases and brought the "Negro League style" to the Majors.

No longer would Dodger players get on base and wait for a slugger to drive them in. The stolen base was again a weapon after years of dormancy.

It's appropriate that the picture that comes to mind when the name Jackie Robinson is mentioned is of him stealing home, for that is how Robinson lived and played baseball. If a base could be stolen, he stole it. The score didn't matter, the inning didn't matter. He struck fear into every pitcher who ever watched him dance off base!

The Yankees beat the Dodgers in the World Series, but the season was still a success and Rickey's experiment was rewarding. Attendance at Ebbets Field grew by 400 percent, and its 1.8 million fans were a National League record.

Robinson was named Rookie of the Year by the *Sporting News*, who stated that their selection was based solely on "stark baseball value."

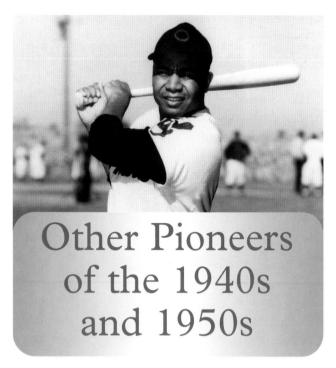

Other Pioneers of the 1940s and 1950s

plate and in the field before being converted to the outfield by manager Lou Boudreau.

Whereas Jackie Robinson was outgoing and aggressive, Doby was shy and introverted. Many believe that Doby was subjected to treatment every bit as horrible as Robinson, he just didn't let the public know it bothered him. Racial abuse got so bad at one point that American League president

There was only one Jackie Robinson, but there were many other barrier breakers. It took many years after Robinson integrated the International League and the Major Leagues, for black players to be seen universally in all leagues, and on all teams across the country.

In late August of 1947, Rickey signed Dan Bankhead from the Memphis Red Sox—the first black pitcher in the modern Major Leagues. Bankhead belted a homer in his first Major League at bat, but was probably past his prime as a pitcher. His Major League record consisted of 52 appearances, a 9-5 record, and a .222 batting average.

One man who doesn't usually get the credit he deserves is Larry Doby, the man who integrated the American League when he joined the Cleveland Indians for 29 games in 1947. Bill Veeck, president and one-third owner of the Cleveland Indians sent his top scout, Bill Killefer, to evaluate Doby, a second baseman with the Newark Eagles. Doby's slugging, though not his fielding, received high marks and Veeck signed Doby and paid Eagles' owner Effa Manley $15,000. Manley was insulted at the paltry sum, but didn't want to stand in Doby's way.

Doby played his last game in the Negro Leagues on July 4, 1947, then joined the Indians in Chicago for a doubleheader. Doby struggled at the

Above: Dan Bankhead became the first black pitcher in the modern Major Leagues when he joined the Brooklyn Dodgers in late 1947.

Right: Larry Doby, the man who integrated the American League, was everything Jackie Robinson was not: quiet, introverted, and insecure.

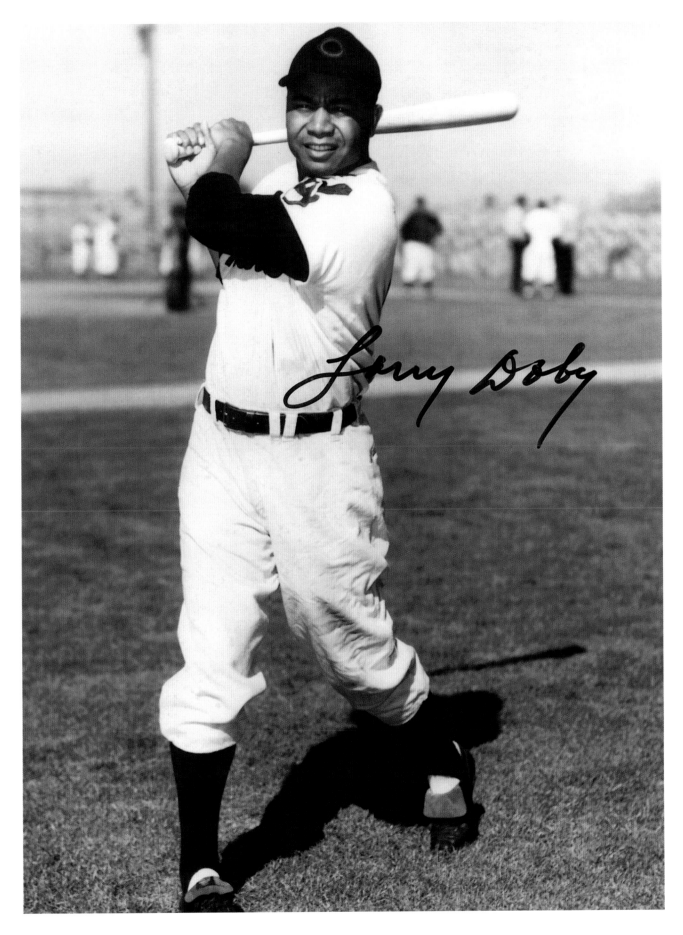

Will Harridge had to talk to several teams about their behavior.

After riding the bench the last month of the 1947 season, Doby was hell bent on making the Big League grade and prove that Veeck's faith in him was well placed. Over the winter, Doby worked on becoming at outfielder with help from Hall of Famer Tris Speaker and, in 1948, Doby became one of the top centerfielders in baseball.

In June, the Indians played the Dodgers in an exhibition game and Robinson took Doby aside and encouraged him. From that day forward, Doby was a star. He helped carry the team to the pennant and ended batting .301 with 14 homers. In the World Series, Doby led the Indians with a .318 average and hit the first homer by a black man in a World Series.

In all, Doby played in seven All-Star games, once hit three homers in a game, hit for the cycle, led the American League in homers and strikeouts twice, and set a record by playing 164 straight games without an error. He was one of only four

Above: Willard Brown (right) was the Negro Leagues' most talented athlete, but failed in a brief stint with the St. Louis Browns.

Right: Hank Thompson flopped with the St. Louis Browns in 1948, but prospered with the New York Giants in 1950.

players to play in the Negro League World Series and the Major League World Series. In 1962, Doby would again break barriers when he and Don Newcombe became the first Major Leaguers to play in the Japanese League.

Two players who didn't perform as expected were Willard Brown and Hank Thompson, both signed by the St. Louis Browns. Brown, 34, became the first black man to homer in the American League, but after only 21 games he left the Browns to rejoin the Kansas City Monarchs. Thompson was only 21 when he joined the Browns, and batted slightly above .250 in 27 games with no homers. He would also leave the Browns, but would return to the Majors in 1949 with the Giants where he would become a solid everyday player.

Star Players of the 1940s and 1950s

On July 9, 1948, the greatest drawing card in Negro League history finally made the Big Leagues. "Satchel" Paige, a man who pitched more games, struck out more batters, and thrilled more fans than any other pitcher, black or white, was signed by Bill Veeck and became the first black pitcher in the American League. Only Veeck knew whether he signed Satchel for publicity or because he thought he could still pitch, but Paige, at least 42–48 years of age, made Veeck look like a genius. Paige's "tryout" is part of baseball folklore, with the ancient pitcher throwing strike after strike over a gum wrapper to manager Lou Boudreau.

Paige went 6-1 in 1948 with a 2.48 ERA and pitched to standing room only crowds, including more than 70,000 in Cleveland for his first Major League start, which he won, 5-3.

That fall, Paige became the first black pitcher to appear in a World Series when he threw two-thirds of an inning in a game five blowout—though historical, Paige was insulted at what he felt was a bone thrown to him by manager Boudreau.

Veeck sold the Indians in 1950 and the team let Paige know he wasn't welcome any longer. When Veeck bought the lowly St. Louis Brown in 1951, his first order of business was to hire Paige again. Paige made the All-Star team in 1952 and 1953 with the Browns, then followed Veeck to the

Portland Beavers of the Pacific Coast League and the Miami Flamingos of the International League. Everywhere he went, Paige drew publicity, but he also pitched well, even into his 60s!

In August of 1956, Paige (50–56 years old) beat Columbus in front of more than 57,000 fans in the Orange Bowl. This was the largest crowd in Minor League history and a week later Paige won his 10th game, against three defeats, and lowered his ERA to 1.50.

In 1965, Paige made it back to the Major Leagues one last time when he pitched three scoreless innings for the Kansas City A's against the Boston Red Sox.

Another big name in Major League integration in 1948 was Roy Campanella, the first black catcher in the modern Major Leagues. "Campy" began his professional baseball career as a 15-year-old with the Negro League's Baltimore Elite Giants in 1937 and over the next nine seasons, Campanella would be tutored by legend Biz Mackey into one of the greatest catchers in Negro League history. In the fall of 1945, Campanella played with a black All-Star team against a Major League team managed by Charlie Dressen and he was soon signed to a Minor League contract with Nassau, New Hampshire, of the Eastern League where he roomed with Don Newcombe and was named league MVP.

Campanella spent 1947 with the Montreal Royals, where he again won the league's MVP award, then started the 1948 season with the St. Paul Saints of the American Association, the first black in the league since Moses and Fleet Walker played in 1883. After tearing up the league for 35 games, he was promoted to the Dodgers where he would become the top catcher in the National League.

Campanella was viewed by some as Jackie Robinson's polar opposite because the two players had very different personalities. Where Robinson refused to accept a single injustice, Campanella was a happy-go-lucky man who got along with everyone it seemed. Campanella, half-black and half-Italian, had a competitive fire equal to anyone, and by 1949 he was the best catcher in baseball. From 1949–1956, Campanella would win three National League MVPs, be selected for every All-Star game,

Above: "Satchel" Paige was often portrayed in print at the time as a shuffling hick from the South, but those close to him knew better.

and set Major League records for home runs by a catcher in a season with 41 and RBIs with 142.

Outside of Organized Baseball, there was integration occurring in semipro circles. In May of 1948, the Southern Minny (Minnesota) League, probably the longest running semipro league, was integrated by Ted "Double Duty" Radcliffe who joined the Rochester Aces. Radcliffe, nicknamed because of his ability as a pitcher and catcher,

pitched well, with a 2.54 ERA, but quit the league when fans in Albert Lea, Minnesota, threatened him.

Radcliffe then jumped to the South Bend Studebakers of the Michigan-Indiana League, the top semipro league in the country and considered

to be Triple-A in caliber due to its many Major League and Minor League stars. Radcliffe, 46 years of age, dominated the league, leading his team in homers and RBIs. He recruited Negro Leaguers Gread "Lefty" McKinnis, a star pitcher from the Chicago American Giants, and Howard Easterling, a third baseman from the Homestead Grays to join the Studebakers.

South Bend and its fans appreciated having top black players and hired Ted Alexander in 1949 and Burnell Longest, Orenthal Anderson, and Walt Thomas in 1950.

1949 brought more black players into the Majors and existing players began to dominate. Jackie Robinson won the National League MVP award with a league-leading .342 average, 124 RBIs, and 37 stolen bases. The best black players to join the Major League ranks in 1949 were Monte Irvin, Don Newcombe, and Hank Thompson.

Thompson, who had flopped with the St. Louis Browns in 1947, batted .280 in 1949 with the New York Giants and by 1950 was an excellent Major

Left: Roy Campanella joined the Brooklyn Dodgers in 1948 and showed that white pitchers could respect a black catcher with talent.

Below: Negro Leaguers were known for their dress as well as their play. Here Roy Campanella and Pee Wee Butts (right) join a friend for a night on the town.

Leaguer with good power. Thompson was the first black player to integrate two Major League teams.

Newcombe spent one year in the Negro Leagues with the Newark Eagles before entering Organized Baseball, and he became the first dominant black pitcher in the modern Major Leagues. In 1949 Newcombe won 17 games for the Brooklyn Dodgers and won the National League Rookie of the Year award. In 1955 Newcombe set a record for most homers by a pitcher (7), and in 1956 Newcombe won the Cy Young award and MVP award.

Before he went into the army in 1943, Irvin may have been the best player in the Negro Leagues, and in 1949 he was still very good. Irvin started the 1949 season with the Jersey City Giants of the International League, before joining the New York Giants in August. In 1950, Irvin batted .299 with 15 homers and in 1951 he led the Giants to their miracle pennant run batting .312 with 24 homers and 121 RBIs. In the ensuing World Series, Irvin batted .458 in a losing effort against the Yankees.

By 1950, the Negro Leagues were gasping for air, with many teams drawing poorly or folding altogether. Fans who once flocked to Negro League games were now willing to drive twice as far to see black players in the Majors. The Negro National League folded after the 1948 season and the Negro American League stopped being a black Major League in the early 1950s. In name, the Negro American League lasted until 1961, but it was primarily a semipro circuit.

Negro League teams tried everything to keep fans coming to the ballpark. The Kansas City Monarchs, Oakland Larks, Indianapolis Clowns, and New Orleans Creole signed women to play, hoping to draw more fans. At least one of those women, Toni Stone, was a legitimate baseball player. Stone, who started her baseball career with the Twin Cities Colored Giants in 1934 as a teenager, was not up to the standards of the Negro Leagues in its heyday, but was still a talented second baseman who would have probably dominated in the

Right: Josh Gibson, the greatest of all black sluggers, died a few months before Jackie Robinson joined the Dodgers.

Left: Don Newcombe, an ace in the Negro Leagues, Minor Leagues and Major Leagues.

All-American Girls Professional Baseball had it not been segregated.

"Boy, she was rough!" remembered Jim Brown, who grew up with Stone. "She could throw just like a man!"

Other "novelties" instituted by Negro League teams included the Clowns lighting firecrackers while the opposing team batted, and the Chicago American Giants signing white players Louis Chirban and Louis Clarizio.

As the 1950s started, there were still 12 of the Major League's 16 teams without a black player. Only the Boston Braves brought a player to the Majors in 1950 when Sam Jethroe made the team

Right: Monte Irvin had some fine years with the New York Giants, but never recaptured his pre-World War II form.

Below: Toni Stone, one of a handful of women to play in the Negro Leagues, wasn't allowed to play in the All-American Girls Pro League.

and won the Rookie of the Year award at age 32 with 18 homers and 35 stolen bases.

Slowly over the decade, each Major League team promoted black players to the Majors. In 1951, Sam Hairston played with the Chicago White Sox. In 1953 there was Bob Trice (Philadelphia A's), Gene Baker, and Ernie Banks (Chicago Cubs); 1954 saw Carlos Paula (Washington Senators), Curt Roberts (Pittsburgh Pirates), and Tom Alston (St. Louis Cardinals); in 1955 Elston Howard (New York Yankees); 1957, John Kennedy (Philadelphia Phillies); 1958, Ozzie Virgil (Detroit Tigers); 1959, Pumpsie Green (Boston Red Sox).

The promotion of Elston Howard was maybe the most important of this list because of the team he played for. The New York Yankees were the

Above left: When Willie Mays was promoted from the Minneapolis Millers to the New York Giants, the Giants took out an ad in a Twin Cities newspaper apologizing.

Above right: Elston Howard, the New York Yankees' first black player, honed his skills with the Kansas City Monarchs.

symbol of Major League baseball and excellence on the field. Yankee's management had first scoffed at the idea of integration. After all, the Yankees won World Series Championships in 1947 and from 1949–1953, while the National League was signing the likes of Robinson, Campanella, Irvin, and Mays.

But the Yankee's cockiness soon ended when its dominance stopped. In 1954, the Yankees won 103 games but the Cleveland Indians ran away with the

Right: Don Newcombe won the Cy Young and MVP award in 1956.

American League pennant. The New York Giants with Willie Mays, the best player in the world, won the World Series in four straight games. It might seem odd for a team to get that upset over losing a pennant, but the Yankees just didn't lose very often in those days.

Elston Howard grew up in the Compton Hill section of St. Louis, where fellow Negro Leaguers "Cool Papa" Bell and Quincy Trouppe grew up before him, and attended Vashon High School, Trouppe's alma mater. Howard paid his dues to get to the Yankees. After playing with the Kansas City Monarchs for three season, Howard was signed by the Yankees and assigned to Muskegon, their Class A team in the Central League. After two years in the army, Howard spent 1953 with the Kansas City Blues of the American Association where he batted .330 with 22 homers, and 1954 with the Toronto Maple Leafs where he led the league with 109 RBIs.

From 1955–1959 Howard backed up Yogi Berra at catcher and played the outfield, but in 1960 he became the Yankee's everyday catcher, and in 1963 he became the first black American League MVP. The National League MVP had been black 10 times already by that time.

Howard had helped the Yankees become dominant again—with Howard in the lineup, the Yankees won 10 American League pennants and four World Series championships in 13 years.

The American League, it seemed, was always a step behind the National League when it came to integration. While the National League Rookie of the Year was black in 1947 (Jackie Robinson), 1949 (Roy Campanella), 1950 (Sam Jethroe), 1951 (Willie Mays), 1952 (Joe Black), 1953 (Jim Gilliam), 1956 (Frank Robinson), 1958 (Orlando Cepeda), 1959 (Willie McCovey), and 1961 (Billy Williams), the American League didn't have a black Rookie of the Year until Tommy Agee won it in 1966 with the Chicago White Sox.

By 1950, it could be argued, black Major Leaguers were simply better than their white counterparts. The reasons can be argued, but the facts cannot. In the 1950s, in the National League, eight

of the 10 MVPs were black (Hank Aaron, Don Newcombe, Willie Mays, Ernie Banks twice, Roy Campanella three). Blacks batted almost 20 points higher than whites, hit about 50 percent more home runs, and stole twice as many bases.

Willie Mays, Ernie Banks and Hank Aaron all started their careers in the Negro Leagues, and all made their Major League debuts in the 1950s— Mays in 1951 with the New York Giants, Banks in 1953 with the Chicago Cubs, and Aaron in 1953 with the Milwaukee Braves.

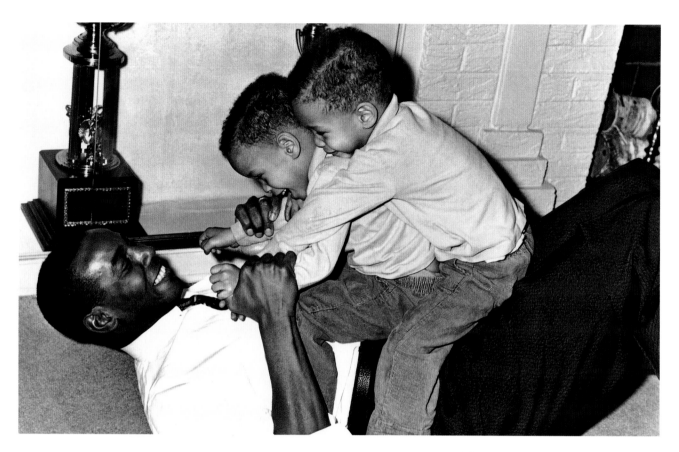

Above: Ernie Banks, the first black slugging shortstop, loved to play!

Many have claimed to have "discovered" Willie Mays, but Mays was so good at such a young age that anyone who watched him play knew he would be a great player. Mays, who grew up in Westfield, Alabama, got his first paying baseball job at 16 from Beck Shepherd, owner of the Chatanooga Choo Choos of the Negro Southern League. After the Choo Choos folded in 1948, Mays was recruited by fellow Alabaman Lorenzo "Piper" Davis to play with the Birmingham Black Barons.

Mays was one of the best defensive centerfielders in the Negro Leagues almost immediately, but it took him a while to consistently hit a curveball. By 1950, Mays was a consistent .300 hitter with power, and was signed by the New York Giants and assigned to Trenton of the Interstate League where he batted .353. In 1951, Mays played 35 games for the Minneapolis Millers of the American Association and there are still people in coffee shops in the Twin Cities talking about his stint. Mays caught everything in sight and batted .477 with a slugging percentage of close to .800! Giants

scouts went scrambling to thesauruses, looking for adjectives to describe Mays. In May, Mays joined the Giants and the club had to place an ad in the Minneapolis newspaper, apologizing for taking away their star.

Mays struggled at the plate for the first few weeks, but after connecting off Warren Spahn for his first Major League homer, he was on his way to one of the most amazing careers in history, and a place on the short-list of "best players of all-time."

In 22 seasons, Mays batted over .300, with 660 homers, 338 stolen bases, 24 All-Star games, the Rookie of the Year award, two MVPs, 12 Golden Gloves, four stolen bases titles, four home run titles, a batting championship, and World Series Championship—all while playing with a flair and exuberance rarely seen.

Ernie Banks started his professional career in 1950 as a skinny 150-pound shortstop with the Kansas City Monarchs under manager Buck O'Neil. In 1953, the Chicago Cubs signed Banks and put him directly on their Major League roster. By 1955, he was the greatest power-hitting shortstop the game had ever seen when he hit 44 homers.

Banks won the National League MVP in 1958 and 1959, despite the Cubs finishing sixth both years. From 1955–1960, Banks hit more homers than any Major Leaguer and in 1962 Banks switched to first base and played another ten years. Banks hit a total of 512 homers with more than 1600 RBIs.

Aaron, like Banks, was a skinny shortstop in the Negro Leagues, who had amazingly quick and powerful wrists. Aaron played part of the 1952 season with the Indianapolis Clowns before being signed by the Milwaukee Braves and being sent to their Northern League team, the Eau Claire (Wisconsin) Bears. Aaron batted over .330 and made such an impression on Midwest fans that more than 40 years later a statue of "Hammerin' Hank" was erected at the Eau Claire ballpark.

In 1953, Aaron had what many consider one of the toughest seasons a black man ever endured when he played for Jacksonville, Florida, in the South Atlantic League ("Sally"). He was one of the first black men to play in the deep South. Aaron went about his playing in a business-like manner, and led the league in virtually every offensive category except, oddly, home runs.

The treatment Aaron received in the Sally League stayed with him throughout his career, and he became one of the leading voices of black athletes, taking over where Jackie Robinson left off.

Aaron joined the Braves in 1954 and switched to right field, joining speedy Bill Bruton, son-in-law of Negro Leaguer Judy Johnson (Bruton would lead the National League in stolen bases three times and triples twice). Aaron hit 13 homers as a 20-year-old rookie and would not hit fewer than 20 homers again until he was in his 40s.

Aaron, many thought, was a candidate to bat .400 because he sprayed long drives to every corner of the field, but he soon learned to pull the ball and, despite weighing only 180 pounds, eventually broke Babe Ruth's all-time home run record.

For many years, Aaron, a reserved man by nature, was ignored by much of the press because of his quiet professionalism. Aaron didn't hit titanic blasts like Babe Ruth or Josh Gibson, and his

highest season home run total was 47, when he was 37-years-old. Year after year though, Aaron hit 30 to 40 homers without much fanfare.

It wasn't until Aaron hit his 500th homer in 1968 that many realized just how great he was. Aaron hit his 600th homer in 1971 and his 700th two seasons later.

As it became obvious that Aaron was not about to slow down, hate mail began to rain down on the star. Aaron received more letters in 1973 than any person in America.

On opening day of 1974, Aaron hit his 714th homer, tying Babe Ruth. Four days later, on April 8, 1974, Aaron hit an Al Downing fastball into the seats at Atlanta Fulton County Stadium and the home run record was his alone. Aaron was much more than a home run hitter, though. He was a 24-time All-Star, a three time gold glove outfielder, an accomplished base stealer (240 lifetime), and a two-time batting champion.

Among Negro League veterans, Aaron is considered, along with Josh Gibson and Ted Williams, as the greatest hitter ever. Aaron retired after the 1976 season, the last Major Leaguer to start his career in the Negro Leagues.

The last group of Negro Leaguers who had success in the Major Leagues included Joe Black, George Crowe, Jim Gilliam, Luke Easter, Sam Jethroe, and Minnie Minoso.

Joe Black made the Major Leagues with the Brooklyn Dodgers in 1952 after eight years with the Negro League's Baltimore Elite Giants and a year in the Minors. Black, a tall hard-throwing right-handed pitcher, was an immediate success in the Big Leagues, winning 15 games, losing four, and saving 15, most in relief. In October 1952, Black beat the Yankees in the opening game of the World Series, making him the first black pitcher to win a Series game.

Although only 29-years-old in 1953, the innings of the year before must have taken its toll and Black's speed and control started to fade. He would figure in only 31 decisions over the next five

seasons, and retired in 1957 at the age of 33 with a 30-12 lifetime mark.

George Crowe and Luke Easter were both large left-handed hitting first basemen: Crowe played his Negro League ball with the New York Black Yankees and Easter with the Homestead Grays. After several terrific seasons in the Minors, Crowe finally made it to the Majors at age 31 with the Boston Braves. The six foot-two inch Crowe played with the Milwaukee Braves, Cincinnati Reds, and St. Louis Cardinals. His best year came in 1957 when he belted more than 30 homers and drove in more than 90 runs. Crowe was one of the top pinch hitters in his final years, retiring in 1961 at the age of 40.

Easter was even larger than Crowe, standing six foot-five, and weighing more than 250 pounds. After a fantastic season with the San Diego Padres of the Pacific Coast League, Easter made the Majors with the Cleveland Indians in 1949. He was 33 years old, although he claimed to be much younger than that.

Left: Joe Black had a short but important career; he was the first black pitcher to win a World Series game.

Right: Minnie Minoso, the ageless wonder, played professionally in five decades.

Easter wasn't fast of foot and was a mediocre fielder, but he could hit the ball as far as anyone in baseball. From 1950–1952, he averaged almost 30 homers and 100 RBIs for the Indians, then played sparingly for two more season in the Majors.

Easter is more famous for his Minor League career than his Major League career as he kept playing until he was 49. He is still a legend in Buffalo and Rochester, New York, because of his great Minor League seasons in the International League with the Bisons and then the Red Wings.

Between the Negro, Major, and Minor Leagues, Easter probably hit more than 500 homers. When he finally retired from baseball, Easter became a bank security guard and was shot and killed during an attempted robbery.

It took a terrific player to move Jackie Robinson from second base on the Brooklyn Dodgers, but Jim "Junior" Gilliam was such a player. A graceful fielder and fine hitter, Gilliam played Negro League baseball with the Baltimore Elite Giants before signing with the Dodgers and spending two seasons in the Minors. Gilliam joined the Dodgers in 1953 and became an offensive spark, walking 100 times and stealing 21 bases on his way to winning the Rookie of the Year award.

Gilliam would play 14 seasons, all with the Dodgers, and would become a Dodger coach upon retirement until he died, just short of his 50th birthday. Gilliam is the only man to hit home runs in the Negro League East-West All-Star game and the Major League All-Star game.

Sam Jethroe made his Negro League debut in 1938, one of only a handful of Negro Leaguers from the 1930s to make the Big Leagues. Jethroe, nicknamed "the Jet," was a fast slashing switch-hitting outfielder who could occasionally fill in as a pitcher or catcher. Jethroe was originally signed by the Dodgers but, while still in the Minors, was traded to the Boston Braves. In 1950, he became the team's first black player. Jethroe was already 32, but, like so many others, "shaved" several years to appear more attractive to the Big Leagues.

Jethroe stole 35 bases and belted 18 homers for the Braves and won the Rookie of the Year. After two more good seasons, Jethroe was traded to the Pittsburgh Pirates where he made one pinch-hitting appearance before being sent to the Toronto Maple

Leafs of the International League where he would play several seasons.

Minoso began his Negro League career in 1945 with the New York Cubans and pinch-hit in the Minor Leagues until 1993. In between he had a terrific career that seemed to last forever.

After four season with the Cubans, the third baseman from Perico, Cuba, played several partial seasons of Minor League ball and had a few at bats with the Cleveland Indians, before making the Chicago White Sox for good in 1951. Minoso would become the heart and soul of the "Go-Go Sox," so named because of the way they manufactured runs.

Minoso was an excellent hitter, batting .300 eight times, but would also take a walk or fastball to the ribs to get on base. Minoso was hit by pitches nearly 200 times in his career. He was also nicknamed "the Cuban Comet" because of his speed, and he would steal more than 200 career bases. In all, Minoso would play in nine All-Star games (two in the Negro Leagues, seven in the Majors), and would win three Gold Gloves.

After his Major League days wound down in 1964, Minoso enjoyed many seasons in the Mexican League, batting over .300 nearly every year. He also played in the Cuban Winter League for several years. He has been inducted into the Cuban and Mexican Baseball Halls of Fame. In 1976, Bill Veeck, owner of the Chicago White Sox, signed Minoso so he could become a "four decade player," and he responded with a single in his second game before retiring again at age 53.

Mike Veeck, owner of the St. Paul Saints of the Northern League and son of Bill Veeck, signed Minoso for one game in 1993. The 70-year-old grounded out in his fifth decade of baseball.

Right: Thirty-two-year-old Sam "The Jet" Jethroe made the Majors after ten years in the Negro Leagues, but was still a top base stealer.

1960s

In the 1960s, black baseball players really took over. Not quite 25 percent of Major Leaguers were black, but in the National League, not only were all home run leaders either black or Hispanic but a white player didn't even finish second in homers in the 1960s. Black players in the National League won the MVP award seven times in the 1960s and won batting titles seven times.

In all of Major League baseball, the top 10 hitters for average in the 1960s were all black except for Pete Rose. Roberto Clemente led all hitters with a .328 average. Others in the top ten included Marry Alou, Tony Oliva, Hank Aaron, Frank Robinson, Dick Allen, Willie Mays, Curt Flood, and Tommy Davis. Hank Aaron hit 375 homers in the 1960s, followed by Willie Mays with 350 and then Frank Robinson with 316.

In the American League, whites still dominated with Frank Howard belting 288 homers in this decade, followed by Norm Cash with 278 and Mickey Mantle with 256.

Roberto Clemente was a magical player with a magical career. It could be argued that he was the "Jackie Robinson of Puerto Rican baseball players." Clemente was the first Major League star from Puerto Rico, and his skin color and the language

barrier, made him often feel like an outsider. The Dodgers originally signed Clemente and placed him on their Montreal Royals Minor League team. The Dodgers tried to "hide" Clemente by not playing him because they felt he wasn't quite ready for the Majors and they didn't want another team to draft him off their Minor League roster, which was within the Organized Baseball rules of the day. The Pittsburgh Pirates, through some clever scouting, drafted Clemente in the 1954 Minor League draft and by 1955 he was patrolling right field for the Pirates like no one before or since.

It was clear from the start that Clemente could field and throw. Fans would come out early to games to watch Clemente warm up his arm with 400-foot throws. To this day, Clemente's arm is the benchmark against which all others are measured. The only question in some people's mind was, "can he hit the curveball?" Clemente answered such questions with 3000 hits, four batting titles, and 240 homers in his career.

Still, many sportswriters thought Clemente to be aloof and moody. Clemente thought he often was overlooked or unfairly criticized because he

Right: Roberto Clemente was as close to perfection on a baseball field as has been seen.

Far right: Roberto Clemente was the first Puerto Rican inducted into the Hall of Fame.

Above: Frank Robinson won the MVP award in the National and American League.

On New Year's Eve of 1972, Clemente flew to Nicaragua with food and supplies for earthquake victims. When the heavy cargo shifted during the flight, the plane crashed and Clemente's body was never found. The Hall of Fame waived its five-year waiting period and Clemente was inducted into the Hall of Fame, the first Hispanic ever to receive the honor.

How does a man win a Triple Crown, an MVP award in both the American and National League, and still be underrated? Frank Robinson never could figure it out either.

Frank and Jackie Robinson had more than their last names in common, each playing with a fire and toughness second to no one, and each speaking out on race issues when others shied away. While in the Minors, Frank let the baseball world know he wouldn't put up with abuse by going into the stands with a bat to shut up a foul-mouthed heckler.

Right: Frank Robinson has carried the torch lit by Jackie Robinson for the last 30 years as a manager and commissioner's office executive.

Below: The Cincinnati Reds traded Robinson to the Baltimore Orioles because "he was an old 30." Robinson responded with a Triple Crown.

was black and Hispanic. For example, in 1961, Clemente led the National League with a .351 average, belted 23 homers, won a Gold Glove, and finished a distant fourth in MVP voting.

Clemente finally won the National League MVP in 1966 when he won his seventh straight Gold Glove, batted .317, and belted 29 homers with 119 RBIs. Clemente played on two World Series champion teams with the Pirates, in the years 1960 and 1971. In the 1960 series, Clemente batted .310, and in 1971 Clemente batted over .400 with two huge homers to win the World Series MVP award. In 1972, Clemente doubled off Jon Matlock for his 3000th career hit, but unfortunately, the Pirates then lost in the playoffs to the Cincinnati Reds.

In the Major Leagues he got into a fight with the Milwaukee Braves third baseman Eddie Matthews in the first game of a doubleheader. Matthews closed Robinson's eye with a punch but Robinson came back in the second game and helped his team win the game.

In 1956, Jackie's last season, Frank made his Major League debut with the Cincinnati Reds and he slammed 38 homers, a rookie record until Mark McGwire hit 49 in 1987. Through 1965, Robinson averaged more than 30 homers a season and in 1961, he won the MVP award with a .323 average, 37 homers, 124 RBIs, and 22 stolen bases.

Before the 1966 season, the Cincinnati Reds made one of the worst trades in baseball history when they swapped Robinson to the Baltimore Orioles for Milt Pappas, Dick Simpson, and Jack Baldschun because, according to the Reds, Robinson was "an old 30." Old or not, Robinson made the Reds look like fools by winning the Triple Crown, American League MVP award, and World Series MVP award. Robinson continued to be a top player until he was pushing 40. In 1975, he became the first black manager in Major League history when he skippered the Cleveland Indians.

Above: Maury Wills didn't make the Majors until he was 28, but he made up for lost time by revolutionizing the running game.

Below: Slight of build, Maury Wills still made the Dodger teams of the 1960s go!

Above left: Lou Brock, the closest thing to "Cool Papa" Bell old timers had seen.

Above right: Cub Fans still bemoan the terrible trade that sent future Hall of Famer Lou Brock from Chicago to St. Louis.

Black players completely dominated Major League baseball in stolen bases in the 1960s, with the top 18 base stealers being men of color, led by Maury Wills with 535 stolen bases. The top white base stealer in the 1960s was Dick Howser with just 94! While Jackie Robinson brought the stolen base back into Major League baseball as a weapon in 1947, Maury Wills made it an art form. Wills studied pitchers and catchers endlessly, until he knew exactly what kind of lead and jump he needed to steal a base.

It took Wills a long time to finally make it to the Majors in 1959, four months shy of turning 27. Wills was a top prospect in 1953 when he barnstormed with Jackie Robinson on a team that included Major League, Minor League, and Negro League stars, but he spent the next few years being overlooked because of his slight build and questionable glove at second base. The Dodgers finally brought him up and placed him at shortstop where he would lead the league in errors in 1960. By 1961, he had worked so hard on his fielding that he won his first of two straight Gold Gloves.

From 1960–1965, Wills led the league in stolen bases every season, and in 1962 he stole 104 bases while being caught only 13 times. Wills was the key to the Los Angeles Dodgers offense, who had few powerful hitters to go with their great pitching. Wills' hitting and baserunning helped the Dodgers win three World Series championships—not bad for someone who weighed a mere 160 pounds. Wills would eventually become a Major League manager with the Seattle Mariners.

Lou Brock took the art of base-stealing to an even higher level during his spectacular career. Brock, a thin and muscular specimen, could run like Wills but also had enough power to hit as many as 21 homers in a season.

Brock debuted with the Chicago Cubs in 1961, but seemed overwhelmed playing right field with the wind and glare at Wrigley Field. In 1964, after three and a half seasons of batting around .250, Brock was traded to the Cardinals and became a .300 hitter and good outfielder. Brock's main job

Right: Billy Williams continued the long tradition of stars from the Mobile, Alabama area ("Satchel" Paige, "Double Duty" Radcliffe, Bobbie Robinson, and Hank Aaron).

though was to make the Cardinals' offense go, which he did. He scored more than 100 runs seven times, led the National League in stolen bases eight times, and bested Wills' single-season mark by swiping 118 in 1974. Brock retired with more than 3000 hits and 938 stolen bases, breaking Ty Cobb's record of 892, which had lasted more than 40 years.

The 1960s saw the sons of former Negro Leaguers make the Major Leagues, including Billy Williams, Cito Gaston, Willie McCovey, and Orlando Cepeda.

Billy Williams might have been the most popular player in Chicago Cub's history if he hadn't played alongside Ernie Banks, but the sweet-swinging slugger could hit with the best. Williams

Left: Brock not only had world class speed, but had enough power to once blast a ball into the Polo Grounds' center field stands, 500 feet from home plate.

Below: Sweet-swinging slugger Billy Williams didn't make headlines, just doubles and homers.

Left: Another of Mobile, Alabama's favorite sons, Willie McCovey learned the game from his dad, a Negro Leaguer of the 1920s.

Above: "Stretch" McCovey blasted 18 career grand slams, second all-time.

was born in Whistler, Alabama, hometown of Negro League standout William "Bobby" Robinson, one of the top fielding third baseman in the Negro Leagues in the 1920s and 1930s.

Williams joined the Cubs in 1959 and became a full-time player in 1961, hitting 25 homers, driving in 86 runs, and winning the Rookie of the Year award. Williams led the National League in games played five times and total bases twice. During the 1960s, Williams hit as high as .333 in a season, hit as many as 42 homers, and drove in as many as 129 runs, but was usually overshadowed by Banks.

Willie McCovey grew up in the baseball hotbed of Mobile, Alabama, which also produced Negro Leaguers "Satchel" Paige, "Double Duty"

Radcliffe, Alec Radcliffe, and "Showboat" Thomas. He joined the San Francisco Giants in 1959, and soon became one of the most feared sluggers in baseball. During the 1960s, McCovey hit more than 40 homers twice and drove in more than 100 runs three times. In 1969, McCovey won the MVP award with a .320 average, 45 homers, and 126 RBIs.

Orlando Cepeda, nicknamed "the Baby Bull," was the son of Negro League shortstop Perucho "the Bull" Cepeda. Perucho, a 200-pound slugger, played briefly in the Negro Leagues, but spent most of his prime years playing in his native Puerto Rico, winning back-to-back batting titles in that country in the late 1930s. Twenty years later, Orlando would repeat his father's feat by also winning back-to-back batting titles in Puerto Rico. Cepeda was inducted into the Puerto Rican Hall of Fame in 1993 and the National Hall of Fame in Cooperstown in 1999. He was the second Puerto Rican to be inducted.

Other Stars of the 1960s

When discussing longball hitters, Willie Stargell ranks with Mickey Mantle and Josh Gibson on a list of the longest hitters ever. Standing six-foot-two and weighing 230 pounds, the left-handed-hitting Stargell pumped his bat at pitchers, then smashed balls high, wide, and handsome.

Stargell played his entire career with the Pittsburgh Pirates, hitting 475 homers over 21 seasons. It was the distance his homers traveled, though, that many remember. Stargell hit two homers completely out of Dodger Stadium (one of two men to do so), hit seven balls over the roof at Forbes Field, and hit four into the upper deck at Three Rivers Stadium.

There were so many great black players in the 1960s that they can't all be covered in a single book, but one player that deserves special mention is Bill White. White homered in his first Major League at bat and was one of the best first baseman in the 1960s, hitting more than 20 homers six times in the decade and winning seven Gold Gloves.

It was after his playing career ended, though, that White really had his greatest accomplishments. In the 1970s, White became an excellent television broadcaster for New York Yankees' games. Then, in 1989, he was named National League President, making him the highest ranking black executive in

all of sports. White retired from the position in 1993 but still works in the Commissioner's office.

Pitching has always been an interesting topic in reference to integration. The stereotype perpetuated for years by Organized Baseball was that black people weren't intelligent enough to be top pitchers, just as it was assumed that they couldn't successfully play quarterback in football.

The fact that Negro League teams, by virtue of superior pitching, had routinely beaten Major League teams in exhibitions for 40 years seemed irrelevant to many white general managers. It is not completely surprising that, while black players dominated baseball offensively, it took longer for them to also dominate on the mound, because they simply weren't given many chances.

If you look at the league leaders among pitchers in the 1960s, it was white pitchers such as Robin Roberts, Whitey Ford, Jim Bunning, Early Wynn, Lew Burdette, Warren Spahn, Bob Friend, Don Drysdale, and Sandy Koufax who were usually in the top 10 in wins, ERA, and strikeouts.

Right: Bill White made the transition from star player, to broadcaster, to National League president; he always wanted to be a doctor!

The lone star pitcher of color in the American League in the 1960s was Camilo Pasquel. Pasquel, a native of Havana, Cuba, joined the lowly Washington Senators in 1954 at age 20. Had he played for the Yankees, his name might be as recognizable as other great pitchers of his era. But he still had some fine seasons, despite lackluster support from his team. In the decade of the 1960s, Pasqual won 124 games against 92 defeats, and made the All-Star team four times. He led the American League in strikeouts three times, strikeouts twice, and complete games twice during the decade.

Luis Tiant, Jr. deserves mention also, although most of his best pitching occurred in the 1970s. Tiant was the son of the former Negro League star of the same name, and they both were experts at altering their windups to keep batters guessing. They both had great pickoff moves, though Junior was right-handed while his father was a lefty. Tiant, Jr. hit his stride in 1968, dubbed by baseball historians as "the year of the pitcher," and went 21-9 with a microscopic ERA of 1.60.

In the National League in the 1960s, three black pitchers joined the ranks of baseball's best and went on to Hall of Fame careers: Bob Gibson, Fergie Jenkins, and Juan Marichal.

Gibson was the most intimidating pitcher of the 1960s, with great speed, a curveball that turned knees to jelly, and a mean streak like few have ever possessed. While on the mound, Gibson absolutely hated batters and he would knock them down for a variety of reasons: if they dug in the batter's box too long, if they had hit him hard earlier in the game, if the previous batter had homered, or merely to save time if he wanted to put the batter on base.

Gibson grew up in Omaha, Nebraska, and became a top high school baseball and basketball player. He went to Creighton University on a basketball scholarship and even played briefly for the Harlem Globetrotters. Baseball was Gibson's first love, though, and Buck O'Neil, manager of the Kansas City Monarchs, tried to persuade Gibson to

play in the Negro Leagues while still in high school. Gibson instead signed with the St. Louis Cardinals and made the Major Leagues in 1959. By 1963, Gibson was a top pitcher, with an 18-9 record, and he only got better. Gibson had five seasons with 20 or more wins, and two 19-win seasons.

1968 was a huge year for Gibson as he went 22-9, had 13 shutouts, and a 1.12 ERA. During the season he won 15 games in a row and gained the National League MVP and Cy Young Awards. He followed this performance with 35 strikeouts in the World Series against the Detroit Tigers, although

Gibson was sometimes perceived as being hard to get along with, but his teammates knew him as a man who expected a great deal from others, in the way they acted and thought. If someone made a racist remark, or a perceived insensitive action, Gibson was the first person to confront them and he made those around him aware of things they might never have thought of before. Gibson's Cardinal's were one of the first truly integrated teams of the 1960s, with black and white players existing in unison on the field, in the locker room, in card games, and socially. Behind the leadership of Gibson, the Cardinal players began to judge themselves and each other solely on their playing abilities and characters.

Juan Marichal, many Negro Leaguers thought, was a throwback to the old days. Not only was he

Left: Juan Marichal, the "Dominican Dandy."

Below: Marichal won 20 games six times in the 1960s for the San Francisco Giants.

the Cardinals lost in seven games. Gibson was one of the great "money pitchers" in Major League history, winning seven straight World Series games, and two game sevens, in 1964 and 1967. His ERA in World Series games was under 2.00 and he pitched eight complete games. Besides being a great pitcher, Gibson was the greatest fielding pitcher in the National League, winning nine Gold Gloves, and was a great hitting pitcher, belting 24 homers in his career.

Gibson is acknowledged as one of the most important players of the 1960s, not just for his dominance as a black pitcher, which was still quite rare at the time, but in his quest for widespread civil rights in baseball.

Left: Bob Gibson went 7–2 in three World Series for the St. Louis Cardinals.

going to beat you, but he was going to entertain you along the way. Marichal, a native of the Dominican Republic, kicked his leg above his head before delivering from a variety of arm angles.

Marichal's talent was obvious from the start, as he tossed a one-hitter in his first Major League start in 1960. During the 1960s, Marichal won 191 games, while losing 88, for a .685 winning percentage. He made the National League All-Star team every year from 1962–1969.

Fergie Jenkins made his Major League debut in 1965, and won 20 games for the first time in 1967. He would win at least 20 games six more times during his career. Jenkins was one of the stingiest pitchers in history in giving up walks, allowing less

Above: Native Canadian Fergie Jenkins won 20 games six times for the Chicago Cubs and once for the Texas Rangers.

Left: Jenkins was elected to the Canadian Baseball Hall of Fame in 1987, and Cooperstown in 1991.

Right: Jenkins struck out more than 3,000 batters and allowed less than 1,000 walks in his career—the only pitcher to do so.

than two per game in his entire career. Jenkins, though he never played for a World Series team, came up only 16 wins short of 300. Jenkins was born in Ontario, and in 1991 he became the first Canadian-born player to be inducted into the Hall of Fame.

Tony Oliva was one of the last Cubans to come to the Major Leagues before Fidel Castro completely closed Cuba's borders. Oliva, whose real first name is Pedro, used his brother Tony's identification to leave Cuba and he kept the name as his own. He signed with the Twins and tore up the Minor Leagues for two seasons before becoming their full-time right fielder in 1964.

Oliva won batting titles his first two full seasons in the Major Leagues and came in second in his third season (while also winning a Gold Glove for his excellent defensive play). Oliva was among the top three hitters in seven of his first eight full seasons in the Majors, and won his third batting title in 1971 when he was 30-years-old.

American League pitchers often listed Oliva as one of the toughest hitters in the 1960s. Oliva, a free-swinging lefty, could pull an inside pitch out of the park or hit an outside pitch down the leftfield line. Oliva was on his way to a Hall of Fame career when his knees betrayed him. After two major operations, Oliva could only just hobble around the ball field.

In 1973, the American League adopted the designated hitter rule, and Oliva's career was extended a few more years. Oliva, considered one of the smartest hitters of his day, tutored Twins' hitters Rod Carew and Kirby Puckett.

One of the most important barriers broken in the 1960s was accomplished by John "Buck" O'Neil when he became the Major League's first black coach with the 1962 Chicago Cubs. O'Neil was one of the top first basemen in the Negro Leagues from 1934 until the early 1950s when he became a playing-manager. During his playing days, O'Neil was a smooth fielder and line drive hitter along the lines of Mark Grace. O'Neil won two batting titles in the Negro Leagues, played in four

East-West All-Star games, and two Negro League World Series.

O'Neil became a Major League scout with the Cubs in the mid-1950s, and helped sign Ernie Banks and Lou Brock. After O'Neil's stint as a Major League coach, he continued in baseball as president of the Negro League Museum in Kansas City, Missouri, an office he still holds, and as a scout for the Kansas City Royals. In 1998, at age 87, O'Neil was named "Midwest Scout of the Year."

During a recent interview, O'Neil was asked by a young fan what he did after baseball. "After baseball?" replied O'Neil. "There is no 'after baseball.' It's all baseball!"

Right: Minnesota Twins outfielder Tony Oliva won batting titles his first two seasons in the Majors.

Below: Chicago Cubs Gene Baker (second from left) and Ernie Banks were the first black double play combination in the Majors.

1970s

The 1970s were bittersweet for black Major Leaguers, with many ups and downs throughout the decade. While the black players of today owe a debt of gratitude to Jackie Robinson for making it possible to play in the Major Leagues, they also owe a debt of gratitude to Curt Flood for making it possible to become rich while playing Major League baseball.

Curt Flood played the entire decade of the 1960s with the St. Louis Cardinals, where he helped them win two World Series championships. Many thought Flood was the defensive equal of Willie Mays in centerfield and he won seven straight Gold Gloves while batting around .300 most years.

After the 1969 season, Flood, along with Tim McCarver, Byron Browne, and Joe Hoerner were traded to the Philadelphia Phillies for Richie Allen, Cookie Rojas, and Jerry Johnson. At the time, the Cardinals were maybe the best-run franchise in baseball, and the Phillies might have been the worst. Philadelphia fans were especially tough on black players over the years.

Flood refused to join the Phillies and asked Major League commissioner Bowie Kuhn to declare him a free agent. Kuhn declined, so Flood filed a suit against Major League baseball and its reserve clause which bound a player to a team for life. This, in essence, made the players that team's property and Flood argued that this was akin to slavery.

The reserve clause gave Major League owners almost complete power when negotiating contracts. For example, if a player had a good season and wanted a raise, the owner could refuse and the only option the player had was to accept what was offered or quit baseball. Over the years, many players held out when offered less money than they thought they deserved, but most eventually signed because they couldn't make more money doing something else.

Many fans criticized Flood, wondering how a baseball player making close to $100,000 a year could compare his fate to that of slaves. But Flood and his lawyer argued that players should have more control over where they play, and that the reserve clause broke antitrust laws. The fact was, the reserve clause in baseball always did break antitrust laws, but courts had always ruled that baseball depended on it to keep costs down and, besides, "it was tradition."

In January 1970, Flood's case was heard in Federal court and he was denied his antitrust suit against Major League baseball.

Right: Hank Aaron, the most consistent power hitter in history.

Left: Curt Flood, the top defensive centerfielder of the 1960s.

Below left: Flood bucked the reserve clause and made it possible for players to make millions.

Jackie Robinson gave testimony supporting Flood's decision, but few other Major Leaguer's expressed their opinion. Owners wielded incredible power over player's careers at the time and so few wanted to risk being viewed as troublemakers. The Judge who ruled on the case, Irving Ben Cooper, did recommend changes to baseball's reserve clause, with input coming from both the players and owners.

Flood appealed the ruling and the case was brought before the Supreme Court, which he again lost. However, during the Supreme Court hearing, Major League baseball made a grave mistake when it argued that the question of whether baseball should have a reserve clause should be a collective bargaining issue, not a matter for the courts to decide.

In 1975 pitchers Andy Messersmith of the Dodgers and Dave McNally of the Montreal Expos played all season without contracts and declared themselves free agents since the reserve clause only applied to contracted players.

The Dodgers and Expos cried foul and the players took them to arbitration where they were, indeed, declared free agents. Since Major League baseball had argued during the Flood Case that matters involving the reserve clause were a matter for collective bargaining, in 1976 the players and owners signed a new collective bargaining agreement of which free agency was a major component. This stipulated that players could become free agents after six years of Major League service. Chicago White Sox owner Bill Veeck publicly said that the new free agency rules would drive salaries through the roof, but most of his colleagues thought he was overreacting.

In 1975, the average Major League salary was about $30,000; it jumped to more than $50,000 in 1976, and is over $2 million today. All players of today should know and respect the name of Curt Flood. He sacrificed the last years of his career to bring about change and more power to the men, who fans pay their money to see: the players.

Before the reserve clause was challenged, stars like Harmon Killebrew, Carl Yastrzemski, and Roger Maris worked part-time jobs during the off-season to help make ends meet. It is safe to say that the days of players working second jobs is now long gone.

One of the first players to reap the benefits of free agency was Reggie Jackson. Love him or hate him, you couldn't ignore him. Reggie struck out often, spoke his mind, and became a household name in the 1970s by rising to every pressure situation that presented itself.

Jackson led the Oakland A's to American League pennants from 1971–74, and the World Series Championship in 1973 and 1974 (the A's also won in 1972 but Jackson had broken an ankle in the playoffs).

In 1977, Jackson joined the New York Yankees at more than $1 million a year, and announced that he would make the Bronx Bombers champions. His braggadocious style and love for the limelight did not sit well with his teammates who had made it to the World Series the year before, only to be swept in four games by the Reds.

Throughout the year, Jackson battled with teammates, manager Billy Martin, and owner George Steinbrenner. He was shifted constantly in and out of the cleanup spot in the lineup and was switched from right field to designated hitter and back again. Jackson seemed to be able to shut these distractions out of his mind, though. He batted .450 in the World Series with five homers, including three in the final game on three consecutive pitches. In 1978, Jackson batted .462 with two homers in the American League playoffs against the Kansas City Royals, and .391 with two homers in the World Series as the Yankees repeated as champions.

In five World Series, Jackson was one of the best clutch players in history, batting .357 with 10 homers and leading his team to championships four out of five attempts. Jackson would retire with 563

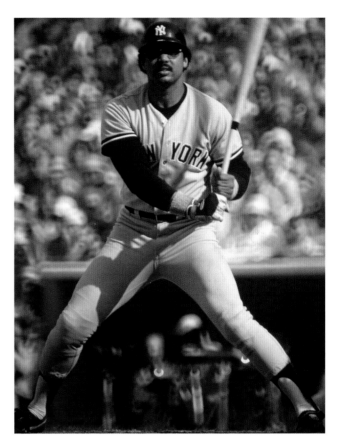

homers, 1702 RBIs, and 2597 strikeouts, which was the most in history.

On September 1, 1971, more than 20 years after Jackie Robinson entered the Brooklyn Dodger lineup, the Pittsburgh Pirates fielded the first all-black line-up: Al Oliver (first base), Rennie Stennett (second base), Dave Cash (third base), Jackie Hernandez (shortstop), Manny Sanguillen (catcher), Willie Stargell (left field), Gene Clines (center field), Roberto Clemente (right field), and Dock Ellie (pitcher).

During the 1972 World Series, Jackie Robinson expressed his wish to live to see a black manager in the Majors. Robinson died less than a month later, on October 24 at age 53. He just missed seeing Frank Robinson become the Major's first black manager in 1976 (and homering as a pinch-hitter in his managerial debut).

Many of the Major Leagues best players continued to be men of color, with black players winning seven of the 10 batting titles in the National League and eight of 10 in the American League.

Rod Carew won six batting titles himself in the 1970s (he had also won in 1969). Carew, a sweet-swinging left-hander, was probably the greatest

Left: Carew's MVP year of 1977 was one of the greatest of all-time: .388 average, 239 hits, 128 runs, 100 RBIs, and 23 stolen bases.

pure hitter of his generation, and even the fact that he played many of his prime years for weak Minnesota Twins teams couldn't keep him out of the national spotlight.

Carew, born in the Panama Canal Zone, was named to 18 All-Star games and was the leading vote-getter many of those years. In 1969, after being taught the art by manager Billy Martin, Carew stole home seven times, which was an all-time season record.

In 1977, Carew almost did what many thought impossible when he flirted with a .400 average. A minor slump in the last weeks of the season left Carew with a .388 average, 239 hits, and the MVP award. It has been said that Carew had the best bat control of any hitter in history, and he could bunt for base hits with two strikes, something other hitters wouldn't even attempt. Carew "slumped" to .333 in 1978, still the league's best, and then was

traded to the California Angels where he finished his career.

To illustrate Carew's batting skill, during a game in the 1970s, Carew's Twins faced the California Angels and Nolan Ryan in his prime. Ryan was throwing so hard that the other Twins batters were shaking their heads, and the pitcher ended up winning the game on a three-hitter; Carew collected all three hits. Carew was elected to the Hall of Fame in 1991, the first Panamanian so honored.

Other top stars of color during the decade of the 1970s included Cesar Cedeno, Ron Leflore, Willie Randolph, Frank White, Bill Madlock, Al Oliver, and Bob Watson.

The Cincinnati Reds of the 1970s, also called "the Big Red Machine," were a melting pot of different nationalities, including many players of color: Tony Perez, George Foster, Dave Conception, Cesar Geronimo, Ken Griffy, Sr., and Dan Driessen.

Perez, a clutch hitter from Cuba, had at least 90 RBIs from 1967–1977, and was an All-Star seven times. He was elected to the Hall of Fame in 2000.

Dave Conception, the second great shortstop from Venezuela (after Luis Aparicio), was the top-fielding shortstop of the 1970s, winning the Gold Glove five times.

George Foster was one of the Red's power threats and in 1977 he hit 52 homers, only the seventh National Leaguer to ever do so at the time. Foster also led the National League in RBIs for three straight seasons, 1977–1979, tying a Major League record.

Ken Griffey, though not as talented as his son would be, was an excellent left-fielder who batted .336 in 1976 with 34 stolen bases.

Only on the Big Red Machine could a man win four consecutive Gold Gloves and be overlooked, but Cesar Geronimo was. The graceful centerfielder from the Dominican Republic was also a decent

Right: Rod Carew was the greatest bunter and pure hitter of the 1970s, batting .343 for the decade.

hitter, batting over .300 once and usually placing among the top National Leaguers in triples.

The heart and soul of the Big Red Machine though was a small dynamo named Joe Morgan. Barely 150 pounds dripping wet, Morgan was a throwback to another peppery infielder from the Negro Leagues: Willie Wells. Both players hailed from Texas (Wells from Austin, Morgan from Bonham), both were small, Gold Glove caliber fielders, and offensive machines.

Morgan broke into the Big Leagues at age 19 with the Houston Colt .45s in 1963. He was traded to the Reds in 1972 and became a superstar. In eight seasons with the Reds, Morgan won two MVP awards, five gold gloves, and made the All-Star team every year.

While most gloves have gotten bigger as the years have passed, Morgan used an unusually small one that looked like it belonged in another era. He used it to his advantage though, by becoming a master at turning the double play.

An exciting player, Morgan flapped his left arm before lashing at pitches (a timing device), ran the bases with speed and daring, and hit 266 homers as a second baseman, the Major League record until Ryne Sandberg broke it during the 1990s.

Rarely in Major League history had such a slick-fielding second baseman provided so much batting punch. Morgan hit as many as 27 homers, drove in as many as 111 runs, scored 100 runs or more eight times, all while stealing almost 700 career bases.

Morgan was elected to the Hall of Fame in 1990. Wells, who retired 10 years before Morgan started, entered the Hall of Fame in 1997. Morgan is now one of the top baseball analysts in the business, and his name comes up often when discussing potential candidates for the baseball commissioner.

Dick Allen and Bobby Bonds were two enigmatic players who played some of their best

ball in the 1970s. Both players were All-Stars multiple times, had immense skills, could be described as belonging to a new breed of outwardly proud black men, and were traded often.

Bobby Bonds was a rare talent, with great speed, power, and personality. He joined the San Francisco Giants in 1968, joining Willie Mays and Dominican Jesus Alou in the outfield, one of the first and greatest all-black outfields in the Majors. Bonds would win three Gold Gloves in his career, but was more known for his offense. Bonds was like Reggie Jackson with speed. He struck out at least 100 times in eleven seasons, twice topping 180. But when he did put the ball in play, he was dangerous.

Five times Bonds had at least 30 homers and 30 stolen bases in the same season, and he ended his career with more than 300 homers and 400 stolen bases. The main reason Bonds was traded so often (he played for eight teams in 14 seasons) was that it was hard to find a spot for him in the batting order. Because he was such a great base-stealer, managers usually put him near the top of the batting order, but he struck out so often that his on-base percentage was low for a lead-off man.

Dick Allen played for six teams in 15 seasons, and was an All-Star seven times for three different clubs. Allen broke in with the Philadelphia Phillies in 1964 and won the Rookie of the Year award. Allen had seven seasons with 25 or more homers, seven seasons with at least a .300 batting average, and ten seasons with at least 100 strikeouts.

Allen's biggest problems, it seemed, were social. Allen was often controversial and preferred to march to his own beat. In 1969, Allen demanded to be traded from the Phillies, and was a no-show for a doubleheader when management refused. That winter he was shipped to the Cardinals.

Allen often argued that he was paid to play games, not to practice, and managers sometimes had to bend the rules for him since he was so productive on the field. In 1972, Allen was the American League MVP with the Chicago White Sox and he was made the highest-paid player in baseball.

Allen ended his career with more than 350 homers, 1,000 RBIs, and 1,000 runs scored. Great numbers for anyone, but many still thought that he underachieved.

1980s

It is possible that by the 1980s, more than 30 years having passed since Jackie Robinson's Major League debut, that most teams judged players based on skills rather than their race. Baseball was big business and the pressure to put a good team on the field was higher than ever.

In the past, teams could field a team just good enough (or mediocre enough) to bring in enough fans to break even financially. But with player salaries averaging close to $1 million in the 1980s, teams needed to draw fans and secure decent TV and radio ratings to break even. For teams with huge player salaries, drawing even two million fans didn't pay the bills. There were still instances when scouts might shy away from a player because of his race, but those instances became fewer and farther between.

There was a time in American history when any young black athlete who wanted to make a career in sports had only one choice: baseball. But by 1980, young athletes could forge financially rewarding careers in football, basketball, tennis, golf, and hockey, and most young black men were concentrating on basketball and football and leaving baseball behind.

Baseball, once the top choice for black fans in America, was now a distant third, maybe lower, and it seemed the Major Leagues weren't too concerned. There were no significant advertising campaigns in the 1980s to draw black fans back to the game, and though at least half of the "stars" in the Majors were black, less than 20 percent of the fans at the ball park were.

As America's black baseball talent pool was drying up, scouts began traveling abroad more than ever and the richest talent pool was found in the Dominican Republic.

By the 1980s, baseball had been in the Dominican Republic for more than 100 years. It was introduced to the country by Cubans who fled their country during Cuba's "Ten Year War" in the 1870s. In the early 1900s, four teams were formed that still exist today: the Licey Tigers (Tigers del Licey in Spanish), Eastern Stars (Estrellas Orientals), the Eagles (Las Anguilas), and the Lions of the Chosen One (Leon del Escogido).

Baseball in the Dominican Republic hit a peak in 1937 when many Negro Leaguers came to play. Rafael Trujillo, the brutal dictator of the Dominican Republic, was up for "re-election" and wanted the capital city, Santa Domingo (at that time called Ciudad Trujillo or City of Trujillo) to win the baseball championship, hoping that it would help him politically.

Trujillo sent a messenger to the United States with a suitcase of money to secure enough players to help him win the championship. The messenger approached "Satchel" Paige and told him to get any players he needed and he could split the money with them any way he liked.

At first, Paige only brought a few players—"Cool Papa" Bell, Sam Bankhead, and Bill Perkins being the most prominent—possibly thinking he could keep a big chunk of the money and still win. When he got to the Dominican Republic, he quickly realized that Trujillo was very serious about winning. Each game was watched carefully by Trujillo and armed soldiers, and there were insinuations that the Dragons of Ciudad Trujillo had better win, or else!

Paige called on Josh Gibson for further help, and the slugger led the team to the championship game, which they won on a Bankhead grand slam. Because Trujillo had spent so much money and resources on building his championship team, professional baseball took a hiatus in the country until 1951, though the Dominican Republic still fielded some of the top amateur teams in the world.

Right: Six-foot, six-inch Lee Smith used a 95 mile-an-hour fastball to notch 478 career saves, the most all-time.

Baseball became the national sport and the national passion in the Dominican Republic and baseball players might be its most valuable export next to sugar. The Dominican Republic became what the United States was years before, a baseball haven with seemingly every youngster playing in vacant lots, dreaming of playing professionally. When kids showed a talent for the game, they were quickly put with others at the same skill level where they could improve and prosper.

San Pedro de Macoris is a sugar mill town and a poor one, but it has produced more great baseball players in the last 20 years than Los Angeles, Dallas, or Miami.

San Pedro de Macoris, with a population of about 125,000, is known in the Dominican Republic as the "Home of Baseball." The Dominican League runs from October through February (when the sugar season is on hiatus) and San Pedro de Macoris plays its home games at Tetelo Vargas Stadium, named for a Negro League star who hailed from Santo Domingo.

Rico Carty was the first big-name player from San Pedro de Macoris. The slugger retired in 1979 with more than 200 homer and close to a .300 life-time average.

The next crop of Major Leaguers to arrive from San Pedro de Macoris came in the late 1970s and 1980s and included sluggers George Bell and Pedro Guerrero. But the city is more known as a "shortstop factory," producing the slick-fielding middle infielders Mariano Duncan, Manny Lee, Rafael Ramirez, Rafael Belliard, and Tony Fernandez. Fernandez was probably the best of the lot and had the most distinguished career, a seventeen year run, with four straight Gold Gloves in the 1980s, four All-Star game appearances, and four seasons batting over .300.

It's been surmised that because the fields in the Dominican Republic are so rough, with rocks and divots everywhere, that if infielders could field there, the well-manicured infields in the Majors were a piece of cake. Another common trait among Dominican players has been their free-swinging hitting styles. Players such as Bell, Guerrero, and second baseman Juan Samuel usually swung at the first decent pitch they saw, because it was said in their homeland, "you can't walk off the island!"

In 1984, Samuel was a perfect example of the free-swinging Dominican approach to batting: in more than 700 at bats, Samuel hit 36 doubles, 19 triples, 15 homers, stole more than 70 bases, struck out 168 times, and walked only 28 times.

There were some fine pitchers from the Dominican Republic that also made it big in the Majors in the late 1970s and 1980s, including Joaquin Andujar from San Pedro de Macoris and Mario Soto from Bani.

Tony Pena, from Montecristi, was one of the top catchers in the 1980s and definitely the most colorful. Pena was famous for bending his legs and torso in a variety of ways to give his pitchers the lowest possible target to throw to. Pena is now one of baseball's best young managers.

Though not Hispanic, the top all-around player of the 1980s was Dave Winfield, who was very similar in stature and ability to Hispanic Negro League star Martin Dihigo. Winfield was tall, powerful, and graceful like Dihigo, and was multi-talented like Dihigo. Winfield was mainly a pitcher in college at the University of Minnesota (where he also played basketball), but became primarily an outfielder in the Majors.

One of the greatest pure athletes to ever play in the Majors, Winfield was drafted out of college by the San Diego Padres, as well as teams in the NBA and NFL—even though he had never played college football. Winfield was the biggest free agent of the 1980s when the Yankees signed him after he had been an All-Star three times with the Padres. Winfield would make the All-Star team nine of ten seasons in the 1980s and would win six Gold Gloves.

In 1981, Winfield had injuries that limited his playing, but the Yankees reached the World Series against the Los Angeles Dodgers. Winfield then suffered through a terrible slump, singling once in 22 at bats as the Yankees lost. Yankee owner George Steinbrenner laid most of the blame on his high-priced superstar, sarcastically calling Winfield "Mr. September" in contrast to "Mr. October" Reggie Jackson.

Winfield and Steinbrenner never did get along, though Winfield put up huge numbers year after year, usually around 30 homers and 100 RBIs. Winfield left New York for the California Angels in

1990 and signed with the Toronto Blue Jays in 1992. The 1992 season was one of the best of Winfield's career, which is amazing since he turned 40 during the year. Winfield clubbed 26 homers with more than 100 RBIs, and the Blue Jays met the Atlanta Braves in the World Series.

Winfield must have felt like he was reliving history when he slumped through the first five games of the World Series with only one RBI and no extra-base hits. But in the sixth game, with a tie score in extra innings, Winfield doubled in two runs, which stood up as the Blue Jays won their first ever World's championship.

Winfield signed with the Minnesota Twins in the off-season and collected his 3000th hit with his hometown club. Winfield retired in 1995, ending his career with more than 400 homers and more than 1800 RBIs. Five years later, Winfield was inducted into the Hall of Fame.

Baseball is a hard game to figure out sometimes and one player in the 1980s is still difficult to describe. Ozzie Smith was about half Winfield's size, weighing about 150 pounds, and he hit 28 homers in his entire career—an average season for Winfield. Yet Smith had as much impact on a baseball field as anyone.

Smith was born in Mobile, Alabama, and, like Winfield, started his career with the San Diego Padres, making the Majors in 1978. Smith struggled to bat over .250 and clubbed one homer as a rookie.

Joan Kroc, wife of Padres owner and McDonald's restaurant founder Ray Kroc, even suggested that Smith earn extra money in the off season as her gardener. For the next 18 seasons, Smith was the best gardener in baseball—the garden around shortstop, that is.

Smith won Gold Gloves in 1980 and 1981, before being traded to the St. Louis Cardinals where he won 11 more in a row. Not only did Smith make all the routine plays, but made the seemingly impossible, too. Smith's specialty was diving plays

Above left: Shortstop Ozzie Smith won the Gold Glove in 1980 and 1981 with the San Diego Padres.

Left: Smith was the first player to make the Hall of Fame primarily for his fielding, winning 13 Gold Gloves, but batting only .262 with 28 homers.

to either side, after which he would spring back to his feet and use his rifle-like arm to throw out the fastest of runners. Smith had such incredible range that he saved more runs than many batters drove in. Smith, a switch-hitter, worked hard to become a decent offensive player, never trying to do more than his size would allow.

Smith rarely struck out, preferring to slap the ball off the turf and use his speed. He was an excellent base runner, stealing more than 500 bases and making nearly 80 percent of his base-stealing attempts. Smith was also an excellent bunter, and he fitted in well with the Cardinals "small ball" style of play. Smith helped the Cardinals win the World Series in 1982 over the Milwaukee Brewers, and the Cardinals would make the series twice more, in 1985 and 1987.

In game five of the 1985 National League play-offs, Smith homered left-handed, his first Major League homer from his left side (in more than 4000 at bats), to beat the Los Angeles Dodgers. The Cardinals would eventually win the series, though they would lose to the Kansas City Royals in the World Series. Smith was inducted into the Hall of Fame in 2002, the first player to be voted in almost entirely for defensive excellence.

In 1987, during an ABC "Nightline" interview on the 40-year anniversary of Jackie Robinson breaking the color line, Los Angeles Dodger's general manager Al Campanis was asked by host Ted Koppel why there were so few minorities in management positions in baseball.

Campanis answered: "I don't believe it's prejudice. I truly believe that they may not have some of the necessities to be, let's say, a field manager or perhaps a general manager."

How strange that Campanis, one of Robinson's biggest supporters in the 1940s, and a lifelong company man from the team most associated with baseball integration, would still be hanging on to such antiquated notions. Many eyes were opened to the fact that not only were there only a few black managers and no black general managers in Major League baseball, but when such jobs became available very few blacks were even given an interview.

In response to Campanis's statements, baseball commissioner Peter Ueberroth insisted that Major League teams consider black candidates when manager and general manager positions open up. Dusty Baker and Don Baylor were two managers who credit Ueberroth with helping them get managing jobs in the 1990s.

Besides demanding more black hirings in the front office, Ueberroth was known for his hard line on drug users—fining and suspending players harshly and demanding they be better role models. For Ueberroth's integrity he was fired by the owners, who felt he wasn't enough of an "owner's commissioner."

Baseball had another race-related problem in the 1980s and 1990s that lasted about 14 years, or the period of time that Marge Schott was the owner of the Cincinnati Reds. Schott was definitely different from most team owners: she was one of the few women owners in Major League history. She was also unrefined and she publicly said things that usually stayed behind closed doors.

Actually, Schott might have fitted in well in the 1940s or 1950s, but by the 1980s most owners knew enough to keep their mouths shut, even if they were thinking the same things as Schott.

Schott became the Reds' owner in 1985, and in 1990 the team won the World Series behind starting pitchers Tom Browning, Jose Rijo, Danny Jackson, and Jack Armstrong. They also had the best bullpen in the league with Rob Dibble, Norm Charlton, and Randy Myers, and the two best all-around players in the National League, Eric Davis and Barry Larkin, who happened to be black.

Davis, a Gold Glove centerfielder, was probably the best all-round player in baseball, hitting for average and awesome power. Davis reminded old-timers of a right-handed hitting Turkey Stearnes, because both players seemed to produce power that belied their thin frames. Davis hit as many as 40 homers in a season and stole as many as 80 bases.

Larkin, a hard-hitting shortstop, was a throwback to Willie Wells or Dick Lundy—shortstops who could hit for power and average. Larkin, a Cincinnati native like Pete Rose before him, won several Gold Gloves, although he had to wait until Ozzie Smith finally slowed down to be rightfully

Left: Eric Davis combined power with awesome speed, hitting 20 homers eight times and stealing 20 bases seven times.

recognized and he won the National League MVP award in 1995.

What was Schott's reaction to her talented black players? According to a Reds' employee, she referred to them as "million dollar niggers." Schott was an equal-opportunity bigot, though—she owned a swastika arm band and was quoted as saying Adolf Hitler "was good in the beginning but went too far." Schott also made insensitive comments about homosexuals and about the over-weight umpire John McSherry who suffered a heart attack on opening day in 1996.

It seemed that Schott spent most of her time as owner either being fined, suspended, or apologizing for her remarks, although she always claimed she didn't mean to offend anyone.

Despite these examples of white ignorance of black people as potential managers or as human beings, black men continued to dominate baseball in the 1980s and 1990s. In the 1980s, every stolen base title was won by a black player. In the National League, Ron Leflore led the league in 1980, Tim Raines led the league from 1981–1984, and Vince Coleman led the league from 1985–1990.

In the American League, Rickey Henderson led the league in stolen bases every year of the decade except 1987, when Harold Reynolds swiped

Above: Rickey Henderson is the all-time Major League leader in runs, walks, and stolen bases.

Right: The San Diego Padres Tony Gwynn won eight batting titles in the 1980s and 1990s, and compiled a lifetime .338 average.

67 when Henderson played less than 100 games due to injuries.

Henderson and Raines, both leadoff hitters, were very similar players, and their arrival in the Majors was heartening to those who felt football was attracting the world's best athletes. Both Henderson and Raines were built like running backs, with heavily-muscled legs, and both had a chance to play Division-1 football, but chose to play baseball instead.

Henderson and Raines, unlike big base-steal-ers of the past, were powerful hitters, too. Four times Henderson belted at least 20 homers, and Raines won a batting title and finished in the top five in batting four times. Both players were still playing in 2002, Henderson at age 43 and Raines at age 42.

Coleman, the National League Rookie of the Year in 1985 with the Cardinals, did a lot of right things on the field, but made a stupid statement off the field that many will never forget. In 1986, a year shy of the 40-year anniversary of Jackie

Robinson integrating the Majors, Coleman told a reporter that he didn't "know nothing about no Jackie Robinson" and was too busy to think about him.

"That would have been the time I'd still be in jail for killin' him," fumed Norman Lumpkin, a Negro Leaguer of the 1930s and 1940s. "I would have done some harm to him, because if it wasn't for Robinson he wouldn't even have been there!"

Somewhere Jackie Robinson was smiling when Cito Gaston became the first black manager to win the World Series. He won back-to-back titles in 1992 and 1993. Gaston, who had a few outstanding seasons as a player in the 1970s with the San Diego Padres, became a fine Major League batting instructor before being hired as the Toronto Blue Jays manager in 1989. Gaston led the Blue Jays to the American League East pennant in 1989 but lost the playoffs to the Oakland A's. The Blue Jays finished in second place in 1990 and first in 1991, this time losing in the playoffs to the Minnesota Twins.

Gaston's Blue Jays won it all in 1992, beating the Atlanta Braves and in 1993 when Joe Carter's homer in the ninth inning of game six beat the Philadelphia Phillies. Gaston, whose father was a Negro League catcher, is to this day, the only black manager to win it all.

One man who often expressed his thanks to those who came before him was Tony Gwynn, the greatest hitter of the 1980s and one of the top handful of all-time. Gwynn was drafted by the San Diego Padres and San Diego Clippers of the NBA, but chose baseball, won eight batting titles and was an All-Star 15 times. Gwynn never struck out more than 40 times in a season, and he walked more times than he struck out in every season of his career.

The stocky left-handed hitter used a 31-inch bat, a full three inches shorter than the average Major Leaguer. Yet he could still hit the ball in the gaps, enough to belt more than 750 extra-base hits in his career. Gwynn's .338 lifetime average ranks 20th of all time and is the highest in the Majors since Ted Williams retired in 1960.

Other black players that dominated the 1980s included Dave Stewart, Andre Dawson, Lee Smith, Frank White, Lou Whitaker, and Kirby Puckett.

Puckett was similar to no other player on earth. No player did the things he did with such an odd body. Puckett was probably 5ft 7in in cleats, weighed more than 200 pounds, and had small feet. When he ran the bases, he always looked like he might fall over. But on the field, Puckett did everything well from first pitch to last.

Puckett came to the Minnesota Twins in 1984 after a brief Minor League career and batted .296 as a leadoff hitter, with no homers in over 500 at bats. The next season Puckett hit four homers in almost 700 at bats. Who would have guessed what seasons would follow? Puckett blasted 31 homers in 1986, many of which traveled in excess of 450 feet. Teammates weren't surprised as they had seen Puckett blast balls in batting practice. It had just taken some tutoring from Tony Oliva and some experience for Puckett to mature as a hitter and learn to pull the ball.

Puckett didn't draw many walks, preferring to swing at anything near the strike zone, and he ripped 200 or more hits five times. From 1986–1995, Puckett started every All-Star game and won six Gold Gloves as the league's best centerfielder. Puckett often seemed to defy gravity as he hurled his stocky body into the air to rob players of home runs.

Puckett helped the Twins win the World Series in 1987, but it was in 1991 against the Atlanta Braves that Puckett really had his coming out party. In game six, with the Braves up three games to two, Puckett did it all. He robbed Ron Gant of a home run by leaping far above the centerfield fence, then homered in the 11th inning to send the series to game seven, which the Twins won again in extra innings.

Puckett was still in his prime when he was stricken with glaucoma in his left eye, which left him partially blind. Puckett's career ended at age 35 with a .318 lifetime average, more than 1000 RBIs, and more than 2300 hits. If Puckett had not been forced to leave the game, he would have almost certainly collected more than 3000 hits. Puckett was inducted into the Hall of Fame in 2001.

1990s

The 1990s saw a change in the average baseball player, and, possibly as a result, records began to fall. While the average Major Leaguer or Negro Leaguer of the 1920s and 1930s was under six feet tall and around 175 pounds, players of the 1990s began to look more like football players than baseball players. Most players of the 1990s worked out with weights year-round, and emerged with a combined size, strength, and speed that had only been seen once every blue moon in the past in players such as Mickey Mantle, Willie Mays, and Willard Brown.

The first record to bite the dust was Lou Gehrig's consecutive games streak, which Cal Ripken broke in 1995 when he played in his 2131st straight game. In 1998, a record that had been flirted with many times, was absolutely smashed. This was Roger Maris's single season home run record of 61.

St. Louis Cardinal Mark McGwire and Chicago Cub Sammy Sosa each broke the 61-home run mark—McGwire on September 8, and Sosa five days later. McGwire would end the season with the unbelievable total of 70, and Sosa would end with 66 and win the league's Most Valuable Player Award.

McGwire and Sosa couldn't have been more different from one another. McGwire, a California

native, was 6 feet 5 inches, weighed 245 pounds, and could hold his own in any NFL weight room.

Sosa, a shade under six-foot, grew up hitting homemade baseball's in a poor neighborhood in San Pedro de Macoris, the Dominican Republic.

McGwire and Sosa weren't the only players to put up ridiculous statistics in 1998. Ken Griffey, Jr. belted 56 homers and Greg Vaughn hit 50. To put these numbers in perspective, if you went back 20 years to 1978, George Foster led the National League with 40 homers, a number that would place him sixth in the National League of 1998 and tied for eighth in the American League.

Home runs weren't just flying out of the park in record numbers, they were flying farther than ever too. Men like McGwire, Sosa, Griffey, and Mo Vaughn were hitting balls as far as Ruth, Gibson, and Mantle on a regular basis, many exceeding 500 feet. All sorts of theories cropped up: the ball was wound tighter, the ballparks were smaller, the players were on steroids, or the pitching was terrible.

McGwire's 70 home runs seemed to be a total that would not and could not be seriously challenged for decades. It seemed like a once in a

Right: From 1997–2002, New York Yankees closer Mariano Rivera was nearly perfect.

98

Above: Chicago Cubs right fielder Sammy Sosa has broken the 60 homerun barrier three times.

Left: Before injuries caught up with him, Ken Griffey Jr. was one of the top centerfielders in baseball history.

lifetime season in which everything had gone just right. The record stood for three seasons.

Barry Bonds, the man who set the single season home run record, probably the most famous record in sports, was also the best player of the 1990s. He has to be listed with the top handful of players ever to play baseball.

Bonds had already won three MVP awards when he hit 73 homers in 2001, had already stolen over 400 bases, had already won eight Gold Gloves in left field, and already earned a wing in the Hall of Fame. What he did in 2001, though, was absolutely incredible to anyone who knew anything about baseball.

Great players like Babe Ruth, Hank Aaron, and Josh Gibson could be counted on to hit the ball hard whenever a pitcher made a mistake, and many

times they would hit the ball out of the park. In 2001, whenever a pitcher threw a pitch that wasn't absolutely perfect, Bonds hit it out. If a curveball didn't curve, it was gone. If a fastball caught too much of the plate then bye-bye! And, some 177 times during the season, Bonds wasn't given anything at all to hit and was intentionally or unintentionally walked. What made it all the more incredible is that Bonds had never hit as many as 50 homers in a season before 2001, and had led the league in homers only once.

Bonds won the MVP in 2001 (obviously) and repeated this in 2002 when he batted .370 with 46 homers, 110 RBIs, and 198 walks—all at the age of 37!

Bonds, with over 600 homers, has a very good chance of breaking Hank Aaron's career home run record of 755 if he chooses to do so and stays healthy. Here's another interesting fact—Bonds will become the first ever member of the 500 homer-500 stolen base club sometime in 2003, and could possibly have at least 600 homers and 600 stolen bases before he retires. The most stolen bases by a player other than Bonds, with at least 500 homers, was 338 by Bonds' Godfather, Willie Mays.

During the 1990s, the Most Valuable Player award went to a black player six times in the National League, and eight times in the American League. From the 1990s and into the 21st century, black players starred at every position in the Majors. As had been the case since the late 1940s, the fastest and hardest hitting outfielders were usually black, with players such as Torii Hunter, Bernie Williams, Vladimir Guerrero, Andrew Jones, Jacque Jones, Albert Pujols, Manny Ramirez, and Ken Griffey, Jr.

It was in the middle infield, though, that blacks now seemed to dominate for the first time in Major

Above: Yankee shortstop Derek Jeter, not yet 30, has led his team to four World Series Championships.

Above right: In 2003, Jeter became the 11th Yankee captain ever, joining names like Babe Ruth and Lou Gehrig.

League history. As rare as power-hitting middle infielders like Ernie Banks and Joe Morgan had been in the 1950s, 1960s, and 1970s, by the year 2000 there were at least a dozen such players—players at primarily defensive positions who were also dangerous batters. Players such as Miguel Tejada, Alfonso Soriana, Roberto Alomar, Derek Jeter, and Alex Rodriguez are all great-fielding middle infielders who also bat in the heart of the lineup.

Alomar, a winner of 10 Gold Gloves at second base, has a lifetime average over .300 and has hit more than 200 career homers and driven in at least 90 runs four times.

Soriano, a rookie in 1999, belted 30 homers and stole 41 bases in 2002 at age 24, and might well be the best player in baseball within a few years.

Jeter, Tejada, and Rodriguez are all shortstops and are the best offensive players on their teams,

something that has rarely been said about a shortstop besides Cal Ripken, Jr. Since breaking in with the Yankees in 1995, Jeter has consistently batted above .300 with more than 100 runs and 20 or so homers. Tejada, a rookie with the Oakland A's in 1997, has belted at least 30 homers and driven in more than 100 runs the last three season. In 2002, he was the American League MVP.

Rodriguez, nicknamed "A-Rod," is to shortstops what Barry Bonds has been to left fielders, with offensive numbers that seem almost ridiculous. Since entering the Majors at age 18 in 1994, Rodriguez has improved every year, winning a batting title at age 21, and in 2001 signing with the Texas Rangers for the most lucrative baseball contract in history.

From 1999–2002, "A-Rod" has averaged nearly 50 homers and 130 RBIs a season. Early in 2003, "A-Rod" became the youngest player ever to reach 300 lifetime homers, and at the rate he's going, Rodriguez has a good chance to break Hank Aaron's (or Barry Bonds?) all-time record.

Right: Oakland A's shortstop Miguel Tejada is among the new breed of power-hitting shortstops.

A special note should also be made for Nomar Garciaparra. Garciaparra is another slick-fielding shortstop with power and two batting titles to his credit. Garciaparra is light-skinned with Hispanic heritage, and may or may not have been excluded from the Major Leagues before integration.

The last stereotype about black players can now hopefully be put to rest: that blacks don't make great pitchers or catchers. It could be argued that the best pitcher in the Majors in the past decade has been Pedro Martinez from the Dominican Republic. From 2000 through 2002, Martinez has a winning percentage of better than .700, and has won three Cy Young Awards: one in the National League with the Los Angeles Dodgers and two in the American League with the Boston Red Sox. He also finished second in Cy Young voting twice. Martinez has led the American League in strikeouts three times and ERA four times.

Just looking at Martinez, it's hard to figure out where he gets his incredible speed as he stands less than six feet tall, and probably weighs 165 pounds. But like Leon Day 60 years ago, Martinez squeezes every little bit out of his body.

The best catcher of the past decade isn't even debatable. Ivan Rodriguez, aka "Pudge" or "I-Rod," won his first Gold Glove at age 20 in 1992 and followed with another nine in a row! Opposing teams, having been victimized enough by the awesome throwing arm of Rodriguez, now simply won't attempt to steal on him.

Rodriguez, a native of Puerto Rico, can also hit with a lifetime batting average over .300 with between 20 and 30 homers a season. Throughout the last decade, a popular topic of discussion among baseball fans has been, "who would you rather start a team with, "A-Rod" or "I-Rod"—the best all-around shortstop in history or the best all-around catcher in history?"

Baseball has come a long way since the first diamonds were laid out more than 100 years ago, and the game has grown along with America. Major League baseball is now finally the melting pot it always thought it was, with players coming from Central America, South America, Australia, China, Japan, and Korea, among others.

Major League baseball still has a way to go until complete segregation is a reality, until managers and general managers are truly hired based on ability instead of skin color, and until a Major League team is owned by a black man or woman.

The National Security Advisor in George W. Bush's administration, Dr. Condoleeza Rice, has publicly expressed her wishes to be considered for the job of Major League commissioner someday. We can only hope that she is seriously considered.

It's heartening to think that the future will only get brighter for baseball, that kids—black, white, and all shades in between—can still dream of making the Big Leagues, and that Jackie Robinson's sacrifices will never be forgotten.

Left: Alex Rodriguez belted 57 homers and won a Gold Glove in 2002. Could he become the best player ever?

Right: In 2003, "A-Rod" hit his 300th homer, the youngest player (27) to reach that mark.

Negro League World Series

details of the series, and, although his American Giants were nosed out for the Negro National League pennant by the Kansas City Monarchs, he did arrange for the last three games of the series to be played in Chicago.

1924 Negro League World Series

Kansas City Monarchs (NNL) defeated Philadelphia Hilldales (ECL) 5 games to 4.

The first modern Negro League World Series was a great one, pitting the Negro National League's Kansas City Monarchs against the Eastern Colored League's Philadelphia Hilldales.

Right: An engraving of Jose' Mendez, manager, and pitcher for the Kansas City Monarchs.

Below: A Championship Cup celebrating the Kansas City Monarchs' victory in the 1924 Negro League World Series.

There were only eleven Negro League World Series contests in the history of segregated baseball. Again, winning a World's championship always took a back seat to mere survival for many teams.

During the history of the Negro Leagues, teams were often criticized for not reporting their games and statistics to the press. Newspapers such as the *Chicago Defender* went to the extent of almost pleading with teams to call in their scores. Usually teams didn't keep very accurate statistics, and no team was in a hurry to report game scores and statistics if they lost. As a result, at the end of each season, it was sometimes hard to tell who was truly the league champion, and who the leading batters and pitchers were. On more than one occasion, there were arguments that the teams playing in the Negro League World Series were not really the true league champions.

In 1923, when the Eastern Colored League was formed, teams from the East raided the rosters of the West and visa versa, which spawned an antagonistic relationship that lasted for years. Relations between the two leagues were so bad in 1923 that a World Series wasn't played.

In 1924, both leagues saw the potential revenues of a Negro League World Series, and a best-of-nine series was agreed upon, with games at each league champions' park, as well as neutral sites. Rube Foster, as usual, was heavily involved with the

Both teams had won about 70 percent of their league games behind deep pitching staffs. The Monarchs boasted 20-game-winners Plunk Drake, William Bell, Clifford Bell, "Yellowhorse" Morris, ace Joe Rogan, and 40-year-old legend Jose Mendez, who was also the team's manager. The Hilldales countered with 20-game-winners "Lefty" Nip Winters, Red Ryan, submariner Scrip Lee, spitballer Phil Cockrell, and Rube Currie.

Each team also boasted great battery-mates. The Monarchs had the talent of Frank Duncan and Hilldale had Biz Mackey and Louis Santop who shared duties. Santop, at the age of 35, was still a great hitter, and batted almost .400 against all

Left: Joe "Bullet" Rogan, the Kansas City Monarchs top pitcher and hitter.

Right: Frank Duncan was catcher for the Kansas City Monarchs' great pitchers for more than 20 years.

competition during the year. He would hit .333 in the series.

Both teams were also solid on defense, with the Hilldales, managed by Frank Warfield, sporting the best left side of any infield in third baseman Judy Johnson and shortstop Jake Stevens. The Monarchs countered with Newt Joseph at third, Dobie Moore at shortstop, Newt Allen at second, and George Sweatt at first.

In 1924, Rogan and Moore may have been the two best all-around players in the Negro Leagues. Rogan won more than 30 games during the season, and batted close to .400. Moore, whose career would end while still in his prime from a gunshot wound, batted well over .400 and led the league in doubles, homers, and slugging. The big power hitter on Kansas City was Oscar "Heavy" Johnson, who carried 250 pounds under his jersey and clubbed more than 50 homers during the season.

On paper, it didn't look like the Hilldales could hit with the Monarchs, as they didn't have many power hitters. Instead, Philadelphia had great bunters and hit-and-run men like Judy Johnson, Jake Stevens, and leadoff man Otto Briggs. Mackey was the only serious power threat, and he could hit them out from both sides of the plate.

The wild card for the Monarchs, it seemed, was manager Mendez and whether he would play at all. The manager was advised by doctors not to play, as he was recovering from recent surgery.

The series started at Philadelphia's Shibe Park and Mendez sent Rogan to the mound against Cockrell. Rogan pitched and hit the Monarchs to a 6-2 victory. Hilldale quickly tied the series when Winters beat Plunk Drake, 11-0, in game two, and the series shifted to Baltimore. Game three was called after 13 innings, tied 6-6, and Hilldale took the series lead when Rube Currie beat Cliff Bell, 4-3, in game four. Hilldale took a 3-1 series lead in game five at Kansas City's park, when Winters won again, this time against Rogan, 5-3. Hall of Famer Johnson provided the big hit with a two-run homer.

Game six saw William Bell beat Script Lee, 6-5, then Mendez, tired of sitting, inserted himself as a reliever in game seven. He ended up winning a 12-inning marathon.

Game eight will go down in Negro League history as the equivalent of "The Merkle Boner Game," with Santop playing the part of the goat. Before the game, Hilldale's shortstop Stevens begged out of the lineup, reportedly suffering from a case of nerves, so Judy Johnson shifted to shortstop, Biz Mackey went to third, and Santop put on the catcher's gear. Hilldale, with Rube Currie pitching effectively, was up 2-1 in the ninth when Kansas City got two men aboard with two outs.

Light-hitting Frank Duncan popped up to Santop behind the plate to seemingly end the inning, but Santop dropped the ball and Duncan was given a second chance. Duncan hit the next pitch hard towards third, where normally Johnson would have made the play easily, but replacement Mackey let the ball get through him and the tying and go-ahead runs scored. After the game, Santop, once the biggest drawing card in black baseball, was bawled out by manager Frank Warfield, who was best known as the man who bit off Oliver Marcelle's nose in a fight. Santop was reduced to tears and was never the same player again.

Nip Winters won his third series game, 5-3, to tie the series at four games apiece, then Mendez chose himself as the pitcher for the deciding game. Mendez and Script Lee were both at the top of their games and each threw shutout ball for eight innings. The Monarchs finally broke through, scoring five times in the top of the ninth. Mendez shut down Hilldale in the bottom half, getting Mackey, the Hilldale's top hitter in the series, to end the game. The Monarchs were declared World Colored Champions.

The Series was a great financial success, managing to draw crowds of nearly 5000 fans per game. Members of the Monarchs made almost $300 each and Hilldale players made about $200. There was also cash left over to go into the league coffers for the future which made Rube Foster a happy man.

1925 Negro League World Series

**Philadelphia Hilldales (ECL) defeated
Kansas City Monarchs (NNL) 5 games to 1.**

The 1925 series was probably over before it began. It's uncommon for a single baseball player to play such a significant role on a team that winning and losing depended solely on him, but that's what Joe Rogan was: uncommon. Rogan, the league's greatest pitcher-centerfielder-slugger, was hurt in a freak accident at home and spent the entire series on the bench. It seemed the Monarchs could never get over this absence, and the Hilldales beat the Monarchs five games to one, becoming the only Eastern Colored League team to ever win the Negro League World Series.

Rube Currie, a giant for the era at six-foot-five, won the 1925 opener at Kansas City, 5-2, going the distance and scattering nine hits. Currie's great pitching in the 1924 series had been overlooked as his team lost, but after the 1925 series it could be argued that he had performed better than any pitcher on either team, winning three of four decisions, with an ERA around one.

Monarch rookie Nelson Dean won game two, the only win Kansas City would boast, beating Phil Cockrell, then Jose Mendez, who didn't have the same old magic of 1924, lost game three in a 3-1 heartbreaker.

Game four was played in Kansas City again, and Nip Winters beat emery-ball pitcher Plunk Drake who lost all three of his World Series decisions in 1924 and 1925.

The series shifted to Philadelphia and the Hilldales made quick work of the Monarchs with great pitching and Biz Mackey leading the offense. In game five, Currie gave up one run on six hits and Mackey doubled and scored the winning run to win, 2-1.

Game six was a good one, despite temperatures barely above freezing. Philly scored in the fourth, fifth, sixth, and seventh innings, the big blow being Mackey's homer off William Bell. With the score 5-1, the Monarchs put up a fight, scoring once and loading the bases before Bell flew out to end the game. Cockrell was the winning pitcher.

Games drew good crowds, averaging 5000 per game. Attendance at the games was still impressive despite unseasonably cold weather, and there was no reason to think the series wouldn't grow in popularity for years to come.

1926 Negro League World Series

**Chicago American Giants (NNL) defeated
Atlantic City Bacharachs 5 games to 3.**

The Chicago American Giants, the epitome of black baseball, won their first Negro League World Series in 1926. However Rube Foster, the father of the Negro Leagues and the extremely successful American Giants' manager for decades was not on the bench to enjoy it. During the 1926 season, Foster's behavior became unusual and eventually he was confined to a mental hospital from which he would never leave. He died there in 1930.

Dave Malarcher, longtime American Giants third baseman, took over the managerial reigns mid-season and led the team to the championship. It's appropriate, too, that the player most responsible for the American Giants great season was Rube Foster's half-brother, Willie Foster, the greatest left-handed pitcher in baseball at the time.

The Negro National League played a split season schedule with the Kansas City Monarchs winning the first half, and Chicago winning the second. During the season, Monarch's shortstop Dobie Moore was shot in the leg, which might have led to the team's decline in the second half.

The ensuing best-of-nine playoff series has become part of Negro League lore. With the Monarchs leading four games to three, Willie Foster beat Joe Rogan, now the playing-manager, 1-0, in the first game of doubleheader. As the two teams were warming up for the second game, Foster played catch on the sidelines. Rogan approached Foster and asked him what he was doing. "Pitching the second game, too," was the response. Rogan, who had already won two games in the series over Foster, and who was batting over .500 in the

Right: In 1926 Dave Malarcher took over the Chicago managerial reigns when Rube Foster became ill; he led them to back-to-back World Series titles.

postseason, let his ego get the best of him and decided to also pitch again, taking the start away from young star Chet Brewer who was scheduled to pitch. It was a mistake on Rogan's part as the American Giants jumped on the tired pitcher for five runs early, and held on to win 5-0 and capture the Negro National League pennant.

The American Giants met the Eastern Colored League's Atlantic City Bacharachs, led by manager and shortstop Dick Lundy and third baseman Oliver Marcelle, who was the equal of Brooks Robinson defensively.

Foster again played a big role, but other pitchers also shared the spotlight. Game one was called a tie after nine innings due to darkness, and game two was a slugfest with Chicago hammering the offerings of Bacharach's pitcher Red Grier.

In game three, Grier came back and threw a no-hitter, one of the most unlikely pitching feats in history. As in the case of Don Larsen's no-hitter in the 1956 World Series, most would have picked a half-dozen other pitchers in the series to perform such a feat. Not only would Grier lose his next, and last World Series start, but, according to the book *Blackball Stars* by John Holway, he would only win one more game in his entire career before leaving baseball and fading into obscurity.

Game four was also ended in a tie due to darkness, and the Bacharachs took the series lead in game five with a 7-5 win. Foster tied the series by winning game six, and then, after Chicago won two of the next three, he ended the World Series by scattering 10 hits in a 1-0 shutout win over Hubert Lockhart. The Foster family finally had its Championship.

1927 Negro League World Series

Chicago American Giants (NNL) defeated Atlantic City Bacharachs (ECL) 5 games to 3.

The Eastern Colored League followed the Negro National League's lead in 1927 and also went to a split season, hoping to inject more interest in the pennant race, and more revenue from a playoff series. This idea was proven worthless as Atlantic City won both halves and advanced to the World Series without a playoff.

Above: Willie Foster, the best lefthander in black baseball, and ace of the Chicago American Giants.

In the Negro National League, the Chicago American Giants won the first half, edging Kansas City, and the Birmingham Black Barons won the second half. In the playoffs, Chicago won four straight games to capture the pennant and Birmingham would have to wait 16 years to make it to their first Negro League World Series.

The similarities between the World Series of 1926 and that of 1927 are startling. The American Giants again won, five games to three, Willie Foster again won the final game against Hubert Lockhart, and an obscure left-handed Atlantic City pitcher would again throw a no-hitter. In game five of the series, with Chicago leading in games, four to nothing, Luther Farrell threw seven no-hit innings before night cut the game short and lionized the huge left-hander. For the first decade of Farrell's career, he won less than half his games and moved from one team to another. 1927 may have been the only season Farrell won more than he lost, and it could be argued that pitching wasn't his best position as he was a hard-hitting outfielder too. Unlike Grier, Farrell had somewhat of a career left after his no-hitter, playing another seven seasons with mediocre success.

Farrell followed his no-hitter with another gem, winning 8-1, then Jesse Hubbard beat Foster, and it looked like a series after all. But Foster came back the next game and beat Lockhart, 11-4, to make the American Giants the first repeat champions in Negro League World Series history.

The Negro Leagues were at a crossroads after the 1927 season. Though attendance was good and skill level high, without Rube Foster's leadership, the Negro Leagues started to break down.

Foster had always been a strict disciplinarian, imploring black players to be gentlemen on and off the field. He knew that Organized Baseball would always look for an excuse to exclude blacks, and did not want rowdyism to bring the league down. Without Foster, player behavior worsened and physical attacks on umpires weren't uncommon. Scheduling, always an issue, became even tougher, and attendance waned. Black journalists began criticizing Negro League players for lacksadaisical play, consuming alcohol during games, and excessive umpire-baiting.

When the Eastern Colored League folded early in the 1928 season, so did the Negro League World Series, and it wouldn't recommence for another fifteen years. In 1932 there was what was billed as "a colored World Series" but, because the leagues were so broken up due to the depression, it wasn't given a lot of credence. The Pittsburgh Crawfords, winners of more than 75 percent of their games across the country during the year, were challenged by the Monroe Monarchs, for "Southern Honors." The Crawfords won the best of nine series in six games, with the Monarchs only win coming when Barney Morris beat Sam Streeter 2-1. The Crawford's Double Duty Radcliffe beat Hilton Smith in the opener, 7-3, then the Craws won four of the next five to win the imaginary pennant.

The Crawfords then faced the American Giants, for "Western Honors," and they disposed of them, too, and were named "Colored World Series Champions." The Homestead Grays disagreed, having beaten the Crawfords 10 of 19 during the season.

1942 Negro League World Series

Kansas City Monarchs (NAL) defeated Washington-Homestead Grays (NNL) 4 games to 0.

Since 1927, teams and leagues had come and gone, East teams still raided rosters of West clubs, West teams still raided rosters of East clubs, and both

East and West teams were raided by the Mexican League. Despite it all, the 1940s were the boom years for the Negro Leagues, with attendance higher than ever. Negro League baseball was the second or third largest black-owned industry in the United States, employing hundreds, and offering player salaries of from $250 to $1000 per month.

The original Negro National League clawed through the depression years, but started to gain steam at the end of the 1930s, and established itself by 1942 as a strong league made up of the top teams from the East, much as the original Eastern Colored League had attempted years before. Teams included the Homestead Grays, Baltimore Elite Giants, Newark Eagles, New York Black Yankees, New York Cubans, and Philadelphia Stars, with the season split in half.

The teams of the Midwest and South, once associated with the original Negro National League, were now members of the Negro American League, formed in 1937. Teams occasionally came

Below: Hard-hitting pitcher Raymond Brown was a key to the Grays' success in the 1940s.

and went quickly, but the mainstays of this league were the Kansas City Monarchs, Chicago American Giants, Birmingham Black Barons, Memphis Red Sox, and Cincinnati (and soon to be Cleveland) Buckeyes.

The first Negro League World Series in 15 years was such a public relations nightmare that it's surprising that they continued. The Monarchs won their fourth pennant in a row by winning both halves of the Negro American League season, and met the Homestead Grays in the World Series. There was controversy from the start, as the Baltimore Elite Giants won the same number of games as the Grays during the regular season, but had one more loss (something that wouldn't have happened if teams played the same number of games). A playoff between the two teams might have been the logical way to crown a winner, but this never happened and the Grays opened the Series in Griffith Stadium in October.

The series was purely a matter of great pitching beating great hitting, with the Monarchs winning four straight games by lopsided scores of 8-0, 8-4, 9-3, and 9-5, with "Satchel" Paige winning three games and Hilton Smith one.

Actually, there were five games played. Game four was won by the Grays, 4-1, but was thrown out because the winning pitcher, Leon Day, was not a member of the Grays. Besides Day, who was a member of the Newark Eagles, the Grays also used illegal players Lennie Pearson and Ed Stone of the Eagles and Bus Clarkson of the Philadelphia Stars.

The only real drama of the series came in game four when Paige didn't show up for his scheduled start. Jack Matchett started instead and was in trouble in the fourth with two on and two out, when Paige arrived in a clowd of dust (from his car) and was rushed into the game. He fanned the batter, Roy Gaston, then threw hitless ball the rest of the way to seal the championship.

1943 Negro League World Series

Washington-Homestead Grays (NNL) beat Birmingham Black Barons (NAL) 4 games to 3.

The 1943 Series started out strangely again. The Birmingham Black Barons had beaten the Chicago American Giants in the Negro American League playoffs three games to two. They then "borrowed" their catcher, "Double Duty" Radcliffe, who was the league's MVP that season, and used him as their catcher in every game of the World Series. The Grays also borrowed from the Giants, playing infielder Ralph Wyatt. They played him at shortstop for the last few games.

Stranger, still, was the fact that Josh Gibson, black baseball's greatest hitter, was benched early in the series and replaced by Roy Gaston. The benching was a result of Gibson's strange behavior, attributed to many things, including drug and alcohol abuse, and a possible brain tumor.

Left: Lyman Bostock Sr., hard-hitting first baseman for the Birmingham Black Barons, who lost three World Series to the Grays.

Right: Grays' first baseman Buck Leonard helped his team to back-to-back championships, batting .500 in the '44 Series.

Left: Josh Gibson, battling illness, struggled in the '43 series, but batted .400 in the '44 affair with a big home run .

Right: Lorenzo "Piper" Davis, second baseman and powerful hitter for the Birmingham Black Barons.

The series went the full seven games, with a few "exhibitions" in between. After the series, the Grays wanted to extend the series to a best-of-nine affair but Negro National League officials said no.

Although playing in the Major League World Series was always a financial boon to players, Negro League players were off salary during their World Series and instead got a cut of the gate. Although the extra pay was significant to many players, big name players could often make more barnstorming against Major Leaguers in California.

The series was interesting nonetheless, with some great pitching performances and equally impressive slugging. The Black Barons, with great hitters Piper Davis, Lester Lockett, Ed Steele, Tommy Sampson, and Radcliffe could put runs on the scoreboard, but the Grays, with Buck Leonard,

Sam Bankhead, "Cool Papa" Bell, Jud Wilson, and Howard Easterling were equally explosive.

The first two games were pitching duels with Birmingham's Al Saylor winning game one, 4-2, and Homestead's Raymond Brown winning game two, 4-3, when "Cool Papa" Bell singled in the winning run in the 11th inning in front of 7000 fans at Griffith Stadium.

The Grays then won game three, 9-0, and Birmingham won a slugfest in game four, 11-10, despite a Gibson grand slam. The Grays whitewashed the Barons in game five, 8-0, but a seventh game was forced when Johnny Markham beat Roy Partlow in game six, 1-0 in 11 innings, in front of 13,000, the largest crowd of the series.

Game seven was played in front of about 4000 fans in Montgomery, Alabama, and was a great one. The Black Barons were ahead 2-0 with two outs in the eighth when Buck Leonard was intentionally walked to face Gibson.

Although Leonard took a backseat to few in the hitting department, it was almost sacrilegious to walk anyone to get to Gibson, who, despite his troubles, was still a threat, and worse, he was due. Gibson singled, which was probably fine with Birmingham who could have been hurt more, but three more singles followed off the bats of Easterling, Vic Harris, and Bankhead, and the Grays went up 4-2. Homestead added two insurance runs in the ninth and held on to win their first World Championship. It's just too bad more fans weren't in the stands to see it.

1944 Negro League World Series

Washington-Homestead Grays (NNL) beat Birmingham Black Barons (NAL) 4 games to 1.

In the fall of 1944, Philadelphia Stars' owner Ed Bolden and much of the black press, said that the Stars were the "real champs" and should have been

Lorenzo "Piper" Davis.

6-1, despite first baseman Buck Leonard being out sick. To be honest, the Grays didn't lose a whole lot as they inserted the versatile Raymond Brown at first, who was one of the top-hitting pitchers in Negro League history. In his two starts at first, Brown fielded flawlessly and collected three hits.

Before game three, there was an auto accident injuring Barons' players Johnny Britton and Pepper Bassett, but Britton begged manager Winfred Welch to let him play. It seemed he inspired his team to victory as Johnny Huber threw a three-hitter (one hit each to Gibson, Leonard, and Bankhead).

In game four, Raymond Brown almost pulled a Don Larsen (or a Red Grier or a Luther Farrell) when he almost threw a no-hitter. "Double Duty" Radcliffe, now the Barons' regular catcher, singled sharply for the only hit.

13,000 fans saw the fifth and deciding game at Forbes Field in Pittsburgh as Dave Hoskins, Leonard, and Gibson homered to make Roy Welmaker a winner, 4-2. Gibson, thought to be losing his touch the year before, batted over .400 in the series and was never benched. The 1943–44 Grays joined the Chicago American Giants of 1926–27, as the only repeat winners in Negro League history.

1945 Negro League World Series

Cleveland Buckeyes (NAL) defeated Washington-Homestead Grays (NNL) 4 games to 0.

There would be no controversy in 1945 as to who was the Negro National League champion as the Grays won both halves, winning more than 70 percent of their games. In the Negro American League, the Black Barons were very strong again but were edged out by the Cleveland Buckeyes by 3½ games in the first half. The Buckeyes nipped the Chicago American Giants by two games in the second half to advance to its first ever World Series appearance.

The series resembled the 1988 Major League World Series when the slugging Oakland A's were stunned by the Los Angeles Dodgers. No one could

in the Negro League World Series instead of the Grays. Of the available evidence, it's not clear why Bolden made his claim as the Grays had the best record for the first half (the Stars were under .500) and in the second half both teams, along with Baltimore, had 12 league wins.

The Black Barons won both halves of the Negro American League season for the right to play the Grays again, with the surprising Indianapolis Clowns coming in second both halves.

The Grays jumped on Birmingham early, winning the first two games in New Orleans, 8-3 and

NEGRO LEAGUE WORLD SERIES

have predicted that the Grays, a team who averaged almost six runs a game in the 1943 and 1944 World Series, would be held to just three runs in four games.

The Buckeyes were very similar to the 1988 Dodgers in that they had great pitching and didn't need to score many runs to beat teams. Their defense was strong up the middle, led by manager Quincy Trouppe behind the plate, Avelino Canizares at shortstop, Johnny Cowen at second, and Sam Jethroe in centerfield.

Twenty-five-year-old Cuban Canizares, many thought, was a great Major League prospect with his flashy glove and strong arm. The fact that he spoke little English, though, made him a bad candidate and he played only briefly in the Minors when he was in his 30s.

The Buckeyes, though somewhat in awe of the Grays, listened to Trouppe, a 16-year veteran, and

Left: Catcher-manager Quincy Trouppe (left) led his young Cleveland Buckeyes to a sweep over the favored Homestead Grays.

Below: The Negro Leagues' 1945 World Champion Cleveland Buckeyes.

out-pitched, out-hustled, and out-played the defending champs.

The pitching Jefferson brothers, George and Willie, had been the two top pitchers in the Negro American League during the regular season. George, 22, went 11-1 in league games with an ERA under 2.00, and Willie, 41, went 10-1 with a league-leading ERA.

The brothers, almost 20 years separating their birth dates, each continued their success in the World Series, Willie winning game one, 2-1, then George winning game three, 4-0 as outfielder Buddy Armour collected a single and two doubles.

In-between, in game two, Eugene Bremer beat Johnny Wright, who the next season would join Jackie Robinson with the Montreal Royals, becoming the first black pitcher in modern times to play Organized Baseball. Bremer gave up only two runs, and broke a 2-2 tie in the ninth by blasting a two-run double off the right field fence.

With a three-nothing lead in the series, Trouppe gave Frank Carswell the start in game four, knowing he would have all his aces ready for game five. Trouppe looked like a genius when Carswell shut out the Grays and beat superstar Raymond Brown.

What happened to Josh Gibson in the series? many fans wanted to know. Although Gibson had led the league in batting during the regular season at .393, he hit "only" eight homers in 44 league games, a rate that would give him almost 30 homers in a full Major League season. Gibson was overweight, and suffering from terrible headaches, possibly from a brain tumor, and batted below .300 in the series. He would die a year later.

On the other hand, Cleveland's Willie Grace played the part of the 1988 Dodgers' Mickey Hatcher. Hatcher, not known for his power hitting, homered twice in the 1988 series to help beat Oakland. Grace, also an outfielder, drove in some key runs in the four-game sweep, including a home run.

Roy Welmaker, one of the Grays' aces, had led the Negro National League in wins with 12, and gave up only six runs in two games in the series, but ended up with two losses. For many years Grays' pitchers had been spoiled by the fact that if they held teams under ten runs they had a great chance

to win. "Josh Gibson would knock in seven or eight all by himself," remarked one-time Gray "Double Duty" Radcliffe.

Following the series, the teams played an exhibition doubleheader at Yankee Stadium and the Grays won both games by identical 7-1 scores. Some fans complained when they discovered the games had not "counted," claiming they were led to believe the games were part of the World Series.

1946 Negro League World Series

Newark Eagles (NNL) defeated Kansas City Monarchs (NAL) 4 games to 3.

Jackie Robinson spent 1946 playing for the Montreal Royals of the International League, so it seems appropriate that the 1946 Negro League World Series would feature players soon to join Robinson in Organized Baseball. 1946 also was the last year that the Negro Leagues came first in black baseball fans' hearts. Soon fans would be following their black heroes on Major and Minor League teams, and the Negro Leagues started to disintegrate. Newspapers would soon be reporting every at bat and every pitch from Robinson, Campanella, Don Newcombe, Johnny Wright, and Roy Partlow.

The Eagles, owned by Abe and Effa Manley, had fielded strong teams since they were based in Brooklyn in 1935. By 1946, the team was managed by Biz Mackey and was awesome, cruising through the regular season winning nearly 75 percent of their league games. For the first time ever, the Grays played under .500 ball and for the first time in nine years did not win the Negro National League pennant.

The Eagles were led by a young double-play combination of Monte Irvin at shortstop and Larry Doby at second. Soon, both players would move to the outfield, Major League baseball, and the Hall of Fame. The pitching staff was led by Leon Day, who started the season with an opening day no-hitter and would later play Minor League baseball and enter the Hall of Fame. Max Manning and

Above: Pitcher Leon Day (right) made a catch in game seven of the '46 Series that saved the day.

Rufus Lewis, also an eventual Minor Leaguer, were also outstanding.

The Eagles caught Newark's fancy and attendance at Ruppert Stadium was outstanding all season, averaging almost 6000 fans per game.

The Kansas City Monarchs, as usual, were a strong veteran team led by the pitching of "Satchel" Paige, Hilton Smith, Connie Johnson, and Lefty LaMarque, and the catching of Joe "Pig" Greene, a powerful batter who had taken over from manager Frank Duncan as the everyday catcher years before. The Monarchs also boasted the league's top percentage hitter in Buck O'Neil, .353, and the top home run hitter in Willard Brown who belted 13 homers in league games and over 40 overall.

Game one was played at the Polo Grounds and Paige and Smith combined to beat Leon Day, 2-1.

Game two was a different story. At home in Newark, boxer Joe Louis threw out the first pitch, and then Newark punched out the Monarchs, 7-4, in front of more than 10,000 screaming fans. Kansas City's Brown homered in the sixth to give the Monarchs a 4-1 lead, but Doby's two-run homer off reliever Paige led to an Eagles' comeback win.

The Monarchs blasted 21 hits in game three and won 15-5, and the series was evened at two games apiece when the Eagle's Lewis threw a four-hitter for an 8-1 win in game four.

Game five moved to Comiskey Park in Chicago and the Monarchs won, 5-1, when Smith beat Manning. The series again shifted back to Newark where the Eagles needed to sweep the last two games to win the series, which is exactly what they did.

Brown again got the Monarchs going offensively when he homered in the top of the first of game six, and before the side was retired it was

4-nothing. The feisty Eagles, as they had done all year, came right back, scoring four in their half of the first. The gloves were off and the hitters took over; Irvin homered twice, Lenny Pearson once, and the Monarchs' O'Neil blasted a homer and RBI single. When the dust cleared the Eagles had won, 9-7, and forced game seven.

Unfortunately, the 7500 Newark fans would not see the Monarchs best players in game seven as "Satchel" Paige, Willard Brown, and Ted Strong went AWOL, apparently leaving for winter league teams and leaving their team shorthanded.

Rufus Lewis, a rookie who went 9-2 in league games during the regular season, was given the start and Irvin gave him an early lead when he drove in a run in the first inning; O'Neil tied the score in the sixth on a long home run. Johnny Davis drove in two Eagles in the bottom of the sixth, and the Monarchs pulled within one in the seventh.

In the eighth, O'Neil blasted a ball into deep centerfield that looked like another homer, or, at the very least a triple, but the versatile Day raced over and made a marvelous catch to protect the one-run lead, 3-2.

In the ninth, the Monarchs gave it the old college try when Earl Taborn, normally a backup catcher, singled with one out, but he was nailed by Leon Day trying to stretch the hit into a double. Ford Smith, a pitcher, then singled, followed by a Chico Renfroe walk. With the tying run on second, Herb Souell popped out to first base and Ruppert Stadium erupted.

Kansas City actually outscored the Eagles 36-34 in the series and might have won game seven if

Below: Larry Doby, Eagles second baseman, homered off Satchel Paige in game two of the '46 Series.

Left: Kansas City Monarchs centerfielder Willard Brown, the top slugger in the Negro American League, was a no-show for game seven of the '46 Series.

Strong and Brown had been in the lineup, but the Eagles were nonetheless a great story.

Effa Manley, Abe's wife, took over control of the team in 1947, but the team couldn't draw like before and was losing money rapidly. After the 1948 season, the Manleys sold the team and it moved to Houston for a short tenure. The Newark Bears of the International League, once the top team in the white Minor Leagues, also suffered from poor attendance and were gone after 1949. Newark, a great baseball town, was without a professional team for years to come.

1947 Negro League World Series

New York Cubans (NNL) defeated Cleveland Buckeyes 4 games to 1.

Jackie Robinson was in the Majors and most black baseball fans followed his every move. Black newspapers curtailed most of their Negro League coverage and filled space with stories galore of Robinson, Doby, and Dan Bankhead in the Majors.

The Buckeyes, under manager Quincy Trouppe, were back in the World Series after a one-year layoff and faced off against the New York Cubans. It was especially obvious that the Negro Leagues were dying a slow death when no playoff was played in the Negro National League due to disinterest, and the Cubans were named champions despite the Newark Eagles winning the first half pennant.

The Cubans were owned by racketeer Alex Pompez, and the next season the Cubans team became a farm club for the New York Giants. The 1947 edition of the Cubans were led by the pitching of fireballer Dave Barnhill, soon to be the property of the New York Giants, and spitballer Pat Scantlebury, soon to be a Cincinnati Red. The offense was led by third baseman Minnie Minoso, soon a Cleveland Indian, catcher Louis Louden, soon a Minor League star, and Silvio Garcia, who led the league in hits and doubles and was once called the greatest player in the league by Pompez.

IN EVENT OF RAIN, GOOD ON NEXT ANNOUNCED DATE

Game   8:45 P. M.

Sept. 19, 1947   Sept. 19, 1947

UPPER   UPPER
BOX SEAT   BOX SEAT

POLO GROUNDS
FRIDAY NITE, SEPT. 19, 1947

EST. PRICE $1.67   EST. PRICE $1.67
Federal Tax   .33   Federal Tax   .33
TOTAL $2.00   TOTAL $2.00

NEGRO WORLD SERIES

SEC. 29   SEC. 29

N. Y. CUBANS
VS
CLEVELAND BUCKEYES

BOX   BOX

THIS ticket may not be resold or offered for resale at a premium in excess of 75 cents plus lawful taxes.

Above: In 1947, $2.00 could buy you a box seat at the Polo Grounds for the Negro League World Series.

Right: New York Cuban Pat Scantlebury, a Panama native, won his only decision in the '47 World Series.

The Buckeyes were led by speedy switch-hitter Sam Jethroe, the closest thing to "Cool Papa" Bell the league had seen in 20 years. He would become the National League's rookie of the year in 1950 with the Boston Braves at age 28. The pitching staff was depleted, though, as the Jefferson brothers weren't what they had once been—Willie had left the team the year before and George had a sore arm that eventually ended his career. Shortstop Avelino Canizares was gone and replaced by Al Smith, who would play one more year in the Negro Leagues before entering Organized Baseball and eventually a 12-year Major League career.

More than 5000 fans saw the first game at the Polo Grounds pitting the Cuban's Scantlebury against Chet Brewer. Brewer, who had started his Negro League career in 1925, had caught a second wind with the Buckeyes at the age of 40, being selected for the East-West game and chosen by Trouppe to start the series opener. His most important chore during the season had been coaching and fathering youngster Sam "Toothpick" Jones, who would be in the Majors by 1951.

Brewer pitched adequately in game one, but the game ended in a 5-5 tie due to rain in the

Above: Snaggle-toothed Cuban Luis Tiant was past 40 during the '47 World Series, but helped his team to victory.

Left: Dave Barnhill (left) wasn't the imposing figure of Satchel Paige, but he shut out the Buckeyes in game two with a blistering fastball.

seventh inning. Brewer would lose his only decision, in game four, to the Cubans' Lino Donoso, almost 15 years his junior. His student, Jones, would also lose his only decision.

The next night, at Yankee Stadium, the Buckeyes won the first completed series game, 10-7, in front of 9000 fans (in a stadium that held 60,000). Ramon Bragana, the Buckeye's 38-year-old pitcher (from Cuba coincidentally) relieved Vibert Clarke with only two outs in the first inning when the starter gave up four solid hits, then pitched 8-1/3 innings and got the victory when the his teammates scored three in the ninth. The Buckeyes had the momentum going their way as they headed back home to Cleveland for game two, but the Cubans then won the next three games by

lopsided scores of 6-0, 9-4, and 9-2, before trimming the Buckeyes 6-5 in the final game behind a combined pitching effort from Luis Tiant and Pat Scantlebury.

The Cubans captured three of their four victories by coming from behind, and the final game, at the Polo Grounds, showed how much the Buckeye's pitching had slipped in two short years. Down 5-0 in the sixth inning, the Cubans scored one run in the seventh, two in the eighth, and three in the ninth.

Tiant, a crafty left-hander, was the father of Luis Tiant, Jr., who would have a great Major League career with the Boston Red Sox and Cleveland Indians. Tiant, Sr., 40-years-old in the 1947 World Series, had a perfect league record during the season and was selected to the East-West All-Star game, then won one game and helped win another in the World Series. Possibly thinking that he had finally achieved every goal in baseball (or because hundreds of screwballs had made his arm so crooked and sore), Tiant retired after the series.

1948 Negro League World Series

Homestead Grays (NNL) defeated the Birmingham Black Barons 4 games to 1.

Like "Caddyshack 2," the 1948 World Series was like a remake without a lot of the leading characters. The Grays and Black Barons, who had met in the 1943 and 1944 Negro League World Series, clashed again in the last ever such series. The Grays' Josh Gibson was gone, replaced in the order by slugger Luke Easter, though Buck Leonard was still around at age 41, and coming off a season in which he flirted with a .400 average. For the Black Barons, "Double Duty" Radcliffe, Lester Lockett, and Tommy Sampson had all moved on, Piper Davis had taken over the managerial reigns while holding down second base, and his team's offense revolved around shortstop Artie Wilson who batted .402 in his last year in the Negro Leagues. The most promising youngster on the Barons was 17-year-old Willie Mays who patrolled center field.

In the playoffs, the Grays had won three straight from the Newark Eagles to win the Negro National League flag. The Black Barons beat the Kansas City Monarchs four games to three for the American League crown.

The Grays then outscored the Black Barons almost three to one in the five World Series games. The only game Birmingham won, game three, was snatched in the bottom of the ninth when Mays drove out a viscous linedrive single, scoring Willie Greason for the game-winner. The story for the Grays was a boatload of runs led by Luke Easter's slugging, and the pitching of Wilmer Fields.

Easter, in his second professional season, had led the Negro National league in homers, batted over .400, and had been selected for the East-West All-Star game. He blasted a grand slam in game four, the big blow, as the Grays raked four pitchers, Willie Greason, Jehosie Heard, Jimmy Newberry,

Above right: Artie Wilson, batted over .400 during the regular season, but couldn't lead his Black Barons to a World Championship.

Right: Birmingham Black Barons catcher Lloyd "Pepper" Bassett hit for power and average in 1948.

and Nat Pollard for 19 hits. Easter would enter Organized Baseball the next season.

Fields, 26, went 7-1 during the year, made the East-West game, and won his only decision in the World Series giving up only one run. When not pitching, Fields played third base and hit well over .300. Fields got help on the pitching staff from five-foot-two inch lefty Frank "Groundhog" Thompson, an effective relief pitcher. "Groundhog," so nicknamed because, well, he looked like a groundhog, was homely, had a hairlip, and was laughed at wherever he pitched—until he started retiring batters! Thompson was described by one sportswriter as looking like a sweet potato sticking out of the ground.

There were few bright spots for the Black Barons in the series, but one player did shine and that was Alonzo Perry. During the regular season Perry had won 10 of 12 league games and batted over .300. With Major League scouts in the stands, Perry won the Barons only game in the series, 4-3 in game three, and he impressed the scouts enough to be signed to a Triple-A contract with the Oakland Oaks. While the scouts were at the game, they were also attracted to Mays, who they signed

to a Class-C contract with Trenton. Although Perry never panned out as a Major League pitcher, he switched to first base in the Minors and spent more than 10 years in the Mexican League, winning that league's Triple Crown in 1956.

Fans at the 1948 Negro League World Series could probably sense the impending doom of the Negro Leagues as there were almost as many Major and Minor League scouts at the games as there were fans. In name, the Negro Leagues would continue for years to come, but in reality, 1948 was probably the last year that it could be considered a "Black Major League." In 1949 almost all top young black players were going straight into Organized Baseball and the Negro Leagues soon became the home for players too old or not skilled enough to be Major League prospects.

The Negro National League folded during the off-season with the Negro American League absorbing most of the teams. There would be no more Negro League World Series games.

Below: Seventeen-year-old Willie Mays (see arrow) drove in the winning run in game three, the only contest Birmingham would win.

Legends

James "Cool Papa" Bell

Born: May 17, 1903, in Starkville, MS
Died: March 7, 1991, in St. Louis, MO
Inducted into the Hall of Fame: 1974
Positions: Outfield, pitcher
Batted: both
Threw: left
Height: 5ft 11in
Weight: 160lb
Years: 1922–1950
Teams: St. Louis Stars, Detroit Wolves, Kansas City Monarchs, Homestead Grays, Pittsburgh Crawfords, Memphis Red Sox, Ciudad Trujillo, Mexico, Chicago American Giants, Detroit Senators.

For baseball fans not old enough to have seen "Cool Papa" Bell run the bases, mere words probably won't suffice to describe him. "If he hits the ball and it bounces twice," remembered "Double Duty" Radcliffe, "just put it in your pocket, because you're not going to throw him out! If he hit the ball back to the pitcher we'd be yelling, 'hurry!'"

It's often helpful when describing a Negro Leaguer to compare him to a Major League player with similar skills. However, it speaks volumes to Bell's uniqueness that there are no Major Leaguers that can rightfully be compared to him. Only Jackie Robinson came close as far as his daring baserunning style, though Bell was much faster.

Bell used his speed to drive teams crazy:

infielders had to hurry their throws, third basemen had to play dangerously close; outfielders knew that if one of his drives got into the gap it would be an inside-the-park home run for certain!

But Bell wasn't just a speed merchant. He was a graceful center fielder with a sure glove, good arm, and he hit line drives from both sides of the plate. About half of his homers were inside-the-parkers and he was often among the league leaders in that category. In a game in the Cuban Winter League one year, he belted three homers all over the fence, against the New York Yankees' Johnny Allen.

Bell grew up in the Starkville, Mississippi, and was an excellent left-handed pitcher as a teenager. He acquired his nickname after pitching in an important game. He supposedly acted "cool" pitching in front of the big crowd; "Papa" was added later and the name stuck. By the time he was 20,

Right: Bell was one of the Negro Leagues' top gate attractions for 20 years.

Below: "Cool Papa" Bell, the fastest man in baseball history.

Bell had switched to the outfield and he covered more ground than any other outfielder for the next 20 years.

Bell's first great success came while playing for the St. Louis Stars, where he helped the team win the Negro National League championship in 1928, 1930, and 1931. Bell batted leadoff, played center-field, and batted in the high .300s.

The colorful Bell was very popular with Negro League fans, and he played in seven East-West games, batting an uncharacteristic .200 in 30 at bats, though four of those game were played when Bell was at least 39-years-old. He did have one great East-West thrill when he scored from second on an infield out in the 1934 Classic to give his team a 1-0 win.

In his best years, Bell stole from 100-170 bases and batted in the mid-.300s. He was once timed circling the bases in 12 seconds flat, and his time to first base from the left side has only been approached by Mickey Mantle. Bell also took advantage of playing many games with only one umpire by purposely "cutting bases short." There were times he ended up with a triple without ever touching first or second base!

Bell was known as a gentleman off and on the field, though he did get into a fight with a white third baseman while playing in the Denver Post Tournament in 1937. Bell came into third with spikes flashing, a common occurrence in the Negro Leagues, and the two players ended up throwing a few punches at each other. Although he missed the final game (which the Trujillo Stars won to capture the title) due to injuries suffered in the fight, he ended up batting .429, the fourth highest in the tournament.

In 1937, Bell joined several Pittsburgh Crawfords, including "Satchel" Paige and Josh Gibson, on the Ciudad Trujillo team in the Dominican Republic League. Bell batted .318 and helped the team win the pennant for Rafael Trujillo, a ruthless dictator. In his later years, Bell remembered armed soldiers surrounding the field as one of the reasons his team played so well.

Bell joined the Pittsburgh Crawfords in 1932 and stayed with them until 1937. These were Bell's prime years when he was the top leadoff hitter in baseball.

Bell spent four of his prime years playing in Mexico, batting over .300 every season and winning the Triple Crown (highest average, homers, and RBIs) while playing with Veracruz in 1940 with a .437 average, 12 homers, and 79 RBIs. There is no record to indicate how many of his home runs were out of the park.

Considering a great deal of Bell's game was based on speed, it makes his career all the more amazing that he didn't hang up his spikes until he was almost 50.

Against Major Leaguers, Bell batted close to .400, and, in available Negro League boxscores, Bell batted a shade under .340. He won three batting titles in the Negro Leagues, but "gave" them away to young players in the hope it would help them make the Big League since he knew he was too old to do so himself.

Negro Leaguer Merle Porter, who played with Bell on the Monarchs in the 1940s, spoke for many players when he said, "I had idolized Bell all my young life and it was really uplifting to play along with him. He was a sweet guy."

Oscar Charleston

Born: October 14, 1896, in Indianapolis, IN
Died: October 6, 1954, in Philadelphia, PA
Inducted into the Hall of Fame: 1976
Positions: Outfield
Batted: left
Threw: left
Height: 6ft 1in
Weight: 220lb
Years: 1915–1954
Teams: Indianapolis ABCs, New York Lincolns, Chicago American Giants, St. Louis Giants, Hilldale Daisies, Harrisburg Giants, Homestead Grays, Pittsburgh Crawfords, Toledo Crawfords, Philadelphia Stars, Brooklyn Brown Dodgers, Indianapolis Clowns, Cuba.

Oscar Charleston was as good an all-around player as ever graced a baseball diamond—maybe even the best. His hitting skills were compared to those

Right: Oscar Charleston: the power of Ruth and fury of Cobb.

of both Ty Cobb and Babe Ruth because he had a powerful left-handed stroke that he used to hit the ball to all fields. He also could bunt with the best men in the game, as well as being able to hit the ball a country mile.

His ferocious approach to the game was very Cobb-like. He played every game like a war, with no buddies on the field. He had blazing speed and worse for infielders, he didn't slow down as he plowed into bases, spikes flying.

Charleston was known almost as much for his temper as for his playing and he got into plenty of fights over the years. In 1915, he beat up an umpire after a questionable call, and he once ripped the hood off a Klu Klux Klan member. Over the years, in a league known for its tough men, only Josh Gibson, the strongest man in baseball, wasn't afraid of Charleston's temper.

On defense, Charleston played rings around Cobb and Ruth. He played a very shallow center-field like Tris Speaker, and could go back to the fence and get the hardest hit balls. Could he field with Willie Mays? "Oh, yes," said one Negro

League player. "He could play a whole lot more center field than Willie Mays. Mays had a better arm, but no one covered more ground than Oscar."

Charleston was born in Indianapolis, and first showed his baseball talent in 1912 when he played with the 24th infantry team in the Army during World War I. He then played in a league in Manila in the Philippines before returning home to play with his hometown ABCs for $50 a month. He was such an immediate success that he was raised to $350 the next season, one of the top salaries in black baseball.

"We used to go to Victory Field (in Indianapolis) and watch him," remembered Negro Leaguer Will Owen, "The crowd would yell, 'Oscar's up, Oscar's up!' The best hitters I ever saw were Turkey Stearnes, Pete Hill, Cristobel Torriente, and Oscar!"

Bobby Robinson, another ABC player, agreed that he was a great center fielder: "He played a whole lot of center field. Everybody just looked up to him. He was truly great—and I mean he was great! I'd say he was one of the best I've ever seen."

In 1921, while with the St. Louis Giants, Charleston played a five game series against the St. Louis Cardinals and hit five homers. During the year, according to "The Baseball Research Journal," Charleston led the Negro National league in batting (.446), was second in hits (79), first in triples (10), first in homers (14), first in total bases (137), first in slugging (.774), and first in stolen bases (28). All this while he was also playing the best center field in baseball. From 1920–1930, Charleston batted over .400 against all competition.

In 1931, Charleston batted close to .400 with the Grays, and the following season was hired by Gus Greenlee as player-manager of the Pittsburgh Crawfords. Charleston, in deference to younger center fielder Rap Dixon, moved to first base and led the team to a quasi world championship by beating the Monroe Monarchs and Chicago American Giants in a roving "World Series."

In 1933, the 35-year-old "Charley" led the Negro National League with a .372 average.

Left: Charleston led the Negro Leagues several years in homers, batting average, and stolen bases.

Charleston stayed with the Crawfords through 1938 before playing for another 10 years with lesser teams.

Pitcher Connie Johnson remembered Oscar as his playing-manager on the Toledo Crawfords in 1939: "He'd take the whole bat rack and drop them as he goes. He had bats strung out from the dugout to the plate. He'd spit at a couple balls and he'd hit the next one out. I ain't never seen nobody like him, and he was 50-years-old!"

In the famous 1952 *Pittsburgh Courier* poll, Charleston was named to the first team as an outfielder along with Cristobel Torriente and Monte Irvin. Another poll in the 1930s listed Charleston as the all-time top center fielder in an outfield with Torriente and Pete Hill.

Negro League game accounts, scant as they are, make it impossible to know what Charleston's lifetime statistics were. It's safe to estimate, though, that had he played in the Major Leagues he might have been a member of the 3000 hit club, the 500 homer club, and the 500 stolen base club with several Gold Gloves thrown in. Charleston died of a heart attack at the age of 57.

Ray Dandridge

Born: August 31, 1913, in Richmond, VA
Inducted into the Hall of Fame: 1987
Position: Third base, second base
Batted: right
Threw: right
Height: 5ft 7in
Weight: 175lb
Years: 1933–1954
Teams: Detroit Stars, Nashville Elite Giants, Newark Dodgers, Newark Eagles, New York Cubans, Minneapolis Millers, Bismarck Barons, Mexico, Venezuela.

"You could drive a train between his legs," said Negro Leaguers about bowlegged third baseman Ray Dandridge, "but not a ground ball!"

Double Duty Radcliffe placed Dandridge on his all-time All-Star team at third base, along with

his hard-hitting brother Alec. Monte Irvin thought Dandridge was better than Brooks Robinson. Ex-Los Angeles Dodger manager Tommy Lasorda said he was the best he ever saw.

Dandridge moved like a cat, charging everything and throwing to first from dozens of impossible angles. Fans came out to the ballpark early just to see Dandridge take infield.

He was born in Richmond, Virginia, and started playing semipro ball as a teenager, where he met Buck Leonard who was playing semipro ball in North Carolina. In 1933, the Detroit Stars passed through Richmond and played Ray's team, the Paramounts. After the game, Dandridge was offered a contract by Detroit manager Candy Jim Taylor for $60 a month. Dandridge signed and never looked back. Taylor worked hard with the 19-year-old Dandridge, changing him from an under-sized home run hitter to a great line drive hitter.

In 1934, Dandridge signed with the Newark Dodgers and became their everyday third baseman beside player-manager Dick Lundy, one of the league's greatest shortstops.

Right: Ray "Hooks" Dandridge fielded like Brooks Robinson and hit like Paul Molitor.

In 1935, Dandridge, now considered one of the best third baseman in the league, was selected to play in the East-West All-Star game and he belted a two-run single in his only at bat (though he actually played second base in the game). In 1936, the Newark Dodgers and Brooklyn Eagles combined to form the Newark Eagles and Dandridge would play with the team on-and-off for almost a decade.

Dandridge played some of his prime years in Mexico, mostly with the Veracruz Blues team that featured Josh Gibson, Willie Wells, and Leon Day. Dandridge usually batted in the mid .300s south of the border, and won the league's batting title in 1948. Dandridge was voted into the Mexican Baseball Hall of Fame in 1989.

Dandridge was signed by the New York Giants in 1949 and assigned to their farm club, the Minneapolis Millers of the American Association. Dandridge batted .363 and won the league's rookie of the year award, despite being 36. In 1950, Dandridge won the league's MVP award when he batted .311 and led the team to the league pennant.

In 1951, Willie Mays joined the Millers and left for the Majors after a month. Dandridge never did, though—maybe because he was too big a drawing card in Minneapolis.

In the famous 1952 *Pittsburgh Courier* poll, Dandridge was voted the fourth greatest third baseman in Negro League history, behind only Oliver Marcelle, Judy Johnson, and Jud Wilson.

Leon Day

Born: October 30, 1916, in Alexandria, VA
Inducted into the Hall of Fame: 1995
Positions: Pitcher, outfield
Batted: right
Threw: right
Height: 5ft 8in
Weight: 170lb
Years: 1935–1954
Teams: Brooklyn Eagles, Newark Eagles, Baltimore Elite Giants, Mexico, Toronto Maple Leafs.

Along with Hilton Smith, Leon Day was the top pitcher of the mid-30s and early 40s. Day bears a striking resemblance to current pitcher Pedro

Above: Leon Day, the top Negro League pitcher from 1935–1945, and a great hitter to boot.

Martinez and he had every bit of speed and struck out just as many batters.

Day was a great all-around player like Joe Rogan. He could bat in the middle of the order and play a great center field when not pitching. Day didn't have the power of Rogan, but he was a dangerous hitter.

Leon Day's first top-flight club was the 1935 Brooklyn Eagles when he was only 17. He was tutored by "Double Duty" Radcliffe on his pick-off move and the next year, when the team moved to Newark, he became the team's ace.

Day's best season was 1937, when, backed by the Eagles' "million-dollar infield," he was 13-0 in league play and batted over .300. All-Star infielder Sherwood Brewer listed Day, along with Hilton Smith, Don Newcombe, and Wilmer Fields, as the best hitting pitchers in the Negro Leagues. In 1940, Day established the Puerto Rican League record of 19 strikeouts while locked in an 18-inning game that was called due to darkness.

Day appeared in seven East-West games, winning his only decision, and posting an astonishing 0.84 E.R.A, and striking out a record 23 men in 21-⅓ innings. In the 1942 Classic, Day struck out five of the seven batters he faced. In 1941, Day showed his versatility by taking over second base for an injured player and became one of the top players at that position in the league. In 1942, in a game against the Baltimore Elite Giants, Day allowed a single to the first batter, then didn't allow another, while striking out 18, a league record.

In 1946, Day started the season with an opening day no-hitter versus the Philadelphia Stars, then led the Newark Eagles to the Negro National League pennant, and the Negro World Series championship against the Kansas City Monarchs. In the series, Day pitched two games, and helped win the last game by robbing Buck O'Neil of an extra-base hit that could have tied the game.

In 1950, Day traveled north to join the Winnipeg Buffaloes of the Manitoba-Dakota League and was signed in 1951 by the Toronto Maple Leafs of the International League along with seven of his teammates. Day was 35 by then, and his arm didn't have the zip that struck out men by the dozen. He soon returned to the "Man-Dak" League, before finally retiring in 1954.

From 1935 to 1950, Day averaged about 12 league wins a year and more than 20 wins a season when all games are considered.

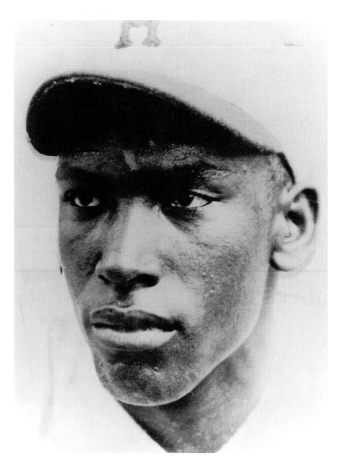

Above: Martin Dihigo could do it all: pitch, hit, run, and throw.

Martin Dihigo

Born: May 25, 1905, in Matanzas, Cuba
Died: May 22, 1971, in Cienfuegos, Cuba
Positions: Pitcher, outfield, second base, third base, shortstop, and first base
Batted: right
Threw: right
Height: 6ft 3in
Weight: 200lb
Years: 1923–1945
Teams: Cuban Stars, Homestead Grays, Hilldale Daisies, Baltimore Black Sox, New York Cubans, Santa Domingo (DR), Mexico, Cuba.

Martin Dihigo may have been the greatest talent to ever grace a baseball field. Buck Leonard thought so, New York Giants' manager John McGraw thought so, and Major Leaguers Johnny Mize and Doc Cramer thought so too. If he had been merely a great pitcher, which he definitely was, he would probably still be a Hall of Famer. But the fact that he was also one of the top outfielders and second basemen in Negro League history, and a powerful batter who often led leagues in batting and homers, made Dihigo a once in a lifetime talent. From the outfield, Dihigo's arm was comparable to those of Roberto Clemente and Carl Furillo, and his power at the plate was similar to Sammy Sosa's. On the mound, the huge Cuban star threw hard, and possessed a great curve.

Dihigo is the only player elected to the baseball Halls of Fame in four different countries: the United States, Cuba, Mexico, and Venezuela. He also threw no-hitters in all those countries except the U.S.

Dihigo first played pro ball with the Havana Reds as a 16-year-old in the winter of 1923 and in the spring he traveled to the United States to join the Cuban Stars as a second baseman. He also spent time in the outfield and by 1926 he was one of the top players in the Eastern Colored League, leading the league in homers in 1926 and 1927 while batting in the .400 range.

In 1932, Dihigo concentrated more on his pitching and he soon became a star, throwing no-hitters in the Venezuelan League three seasons in a row.

Dihigo, despite his great talents, gave up the most famous home run in Negro League history. In the 1935 East-West All-Star game, with the score tied in extra innings, Dihigo came from centerfield to the pitching mound and ended up giving up a 480 foot homer to Mule Suttles.

Dihigo played in Latin countries so often that he only played in the East-West game twice, in 1935 and 1945. In 1937, Dihigo went 4-0 with a 0.93 ERA for Veracruz, then moved on to the Dominican Republic with the Aguilas Cibaenas team. In 25 games he batted .351 (3rd) with four homers (1st), 34 hits (2nd), and six doubles (2nd) in a 31-game season. On the mound Dihigo had a 6-4 record, the second best in the league behind "Satchel" Paige's 8-1, and tossed a no-hitter. In the final game of the season, won by Ciudad Trujillo, Dihigo started on the mound and went four for five at the plate. When he got into trouble in the 5th inning, Chet Brewer relieved and gave up a grand slam to Sammy Bankhead.

In 1938, Dihigo led his team to the Mexican League pennant by topping the league in wins (18), strikeouts, ERA (0.90), and batting average (.387); he also had a six for six game for good measure.

In 1939, Dihigo went 15-8 with a league-leading 202 strikeouts (18 in one game) and batted .336. From 1937–1942, Dihigo batted over .300 every year and led the league in strikeouts on the mound.

In 1940, Dihigo batted .365 with Veracruz, and in 1941 he joined Torreon and batted .319 while leading all pitchers with a 22-7 record with a 2.53 ERA. His last season with Torreon he batted .316 with an 11-4 record.

Dihigo stayed in baseball as a manager in Mexico, Venezuela, and the Dominican Republic before retiring to his home country of Cuba and becoming Fidel Castro's Minister of Sports.

In a 1952 *Pittsburgh Courier* poll, Dihigo was named on the first team as a utility man, and also received votes for outfield, third base, and pitcher.

Rube Foster

Born: September 17, 1879, in Calvert, TX
Died: December 9, 1930, in Kankakee, IL
Inducted into the Hall of Fame: 1981
Positions: Pitcher
Batted: right
Threw: right
Height: 6ft 3in
Weight: 220lb
Years: 1902–1926
Teams: Chicago Union Giants, Cuban X-Giants, Philadelphia Giants, Chicago Lelands, Chicago American Giants.

Foster is the father of Negro League baseball in the modern era, and players of all colors owe him a debt of gratitude for starting the original Negro National League. If it wasn't for Foster, we might never have heard of "Satchel" Paige, Jackie Robinson, or Barry Bonds.

Foster was the son of a minister, and spent time studying the clergy at Tillotson College. He grew up in Texas, and became a star pitcher at a young age with the Fort Worth Yellow Jackets.

In 1901, Foster joined Frank Leland's Chicago Union Giants for $40 a month and a 15¢ a meal stipend. Foster threw submarine style, with a good fastball and screwball, and he was compared in the black press to all the great white pitchers of the day: Cy Young, Adie Joss, and Hoss Radbourne. He beat the Philadelphia A's and their star, Rube Waddell, in a game in 1902 and from that point he was no longer Andrew, but Rube.

As was the case with most pitching stars of the early 1900s, Rube was expected to pitch almost every day, and in his prime he won 50 or more games a year. Foster moved around quite a bit in his playing days, pitching for all the great early teams including the Cuban X-Giants, Philadelphia Giants, and Leland Giants.

It was on the 1907 Leland Giants that Foster first took a crack at managing, and it was obvious from the start that he was born to do so. Foster had a brilliant baseball mind and the ultimate respect of his players. At 6 feet 3 inches and around 220 pounds, Foster let his players know that there was only one boss on the field: Rube!

The Lelands played their home games at Auburn Park at 79th and Wentworth in Chicago and competed in Chicago's tough semipro circuit as the only black team. It's interesting to note that one of the league's other teams was the Chicago Colts, run by Cap Anson, known as the man who drew the original color line.

The 1907 Lelands won 110 of 120 games, including 48 in a row, then continued to thrive. In 1910, with players Pop Lloyd, "Homerun" Johnson, Frank Wickware, Pat Dougherty, Bruce Petway, and Pete Hill, the Lelands won 123 of 129 games. In 1911, Foster bought ownership in "Old White Sox Park" at 39th and Wentworth when the White Sox moved to Comiskey Park, and renamed the team the Chicago American Giants. For the next 15 years, Foster revolutionized black baseball.

Foster was well respected by Organized Baseball, and New York Giants' manager John McGraw, his good friend, hired Foster one spring to coach pitcher Christy Matthewson. Foster's teams put the fear of God into every opponent, by

Above: Rube Foster (right) with Cap Anson, the man who drew baseball's color line.

Right: Rube Foster, the father of the modern Negro Leagues.

playing the most daring style of baseball every seen. Every player was expected to be able to bunt, run, and think on his feet.

"Sometimes they'd bunt all the way through the lineup," remembered "Double Duty" Radcliffe, who pitched batting practice to the Chicago American Giants in 1919. "They could score ten runs and the ball never leaves the infield. Looked like a track meet!"

Foster was known to make strange wagers on games, such as betting opposing teams that his American Giants could win a game on a steal of home or could win without hitting a ball into the outfield.

In 1920, Foster and other owners of black teams, met at the Paseo "Colored" YMCA in

Kansas City, and formed the Negro National League, because, in Foster's words, he wanted to "keep Colored baseball from the control of Whites, and to do something for the loyalty of the Race."

Foster was the czar of the new league, stationed at his office at Indiana and Wentworth in Chicago, and had his hand in almost every detail of its operation. To provide competitive balance, Foster would often shift players from one team to another, including moving superstar Oscar Charleston from his own team to the Indianapolis ABCs. He also lent money to teams in trouble, knowing that a league was only as strong as its weakest franchise.

Foster also laid down the ground rules that he expected all players to follow. Foster demanded that all Negro League players conduct themselves in a "Big League" fashion in their manners, conduct, and dress. Only with first class ballplayers did Foster think that Organized Baseball would ever be integrated. It was Foster's vision, though, that entire Negro League teams would eventually enter into the Major Leagues—this was a dream that was never realized.

When the Eastern Colored League was formed in 1923, Foster was confronted with his first crisis when Eastern teams raided his league's team rosters. He responded by forming relationships with Eastern owners, knowing it would mean more revenue and success for all, and in 1924 the first Negro League World Series was played with the Kansas City Monarchs beating the Philadelphia Hilldales. Two years later, in 1926, the Chicago American Giants won the Negro National League pennant and beat the Atlantic City Bacharachs in the World Series.

Foster, however, was unable to enjoy the victory as he had been placed into an insane asylum in Kankakee, Illinois, mid-season after a mental breakdown. He was replaced as manager by Dave Malarcher. The American Giants would again beat Atlantic City in the 1927 World Series before the Eastern Colored League folded.

The next few years were very lean ones for black baseball, and the reason seems obvious. Without Foster's guidance, Negro League baseball had no strong leadership, and was basically a lawless entity. Rube Foster died on December 8, 1930, after spending his last four years in hospital.

THE GREATS

Josh Gibson

Born: December 21, 1911, in Buena Vista, GA
Died: January 20, 1947, in Pittsburgh, PA
Inducted into the Hall of Fame: 1972
Positions: Catcher, outfield
Batted: right
Threw: right
Height: 6ft 1in
Weight: 225lb
Teams: Pittsburgh Crawfords, Homestead Grays, Ciudad Trujillo (Dominican Republic), Mexico City.

Imagine Paul Molitor, with his short stride, compact swing, and lightening reflexes, and then add 40 pounds of muscle—that was Josh Gibson. Like Molitor, Gibson had no weaknesses at the plate, but unlike Molitor, he also had a legendary strength matched only by Mickey Mantle. The kind of strength that authored 500 foot home runs. It shouldn't be surprising, then, that Gibson is a member of an elite group of men (including Ted Williams, Hank Aaron, and Babe Ruth) who have arguably been called "the greatest hitter ever."

It would take years of research to figure out how many homers Gibson really hit, but the number is at least in the 700 range, if not 1000. Granted, he hit many of these against semipros not of Major League caliber, but against Major

Leaguers he proved he was the real deal by blasting homers off the greatest pitchers they had to offer. In East-West All-Star games, against the best Negro League pitchers, he batted .483.

Buck O'Neil, Negro League superstar, first baseman, and manager, thought Gibson's power was equal to that of Babe Ruth's, but while Ruth struck out more than 100 times per season, Gibson struck out around 20 times per season.

Gibson ran well until catching doubleheaders caught up with his knees, had a great arm, and loved to play. "He was just like a little kid on the field," one player remembered. "We'd all be tired after playing two or three games in one day. Josh would have kept on playing!"

Some will argue that Gibson wasn't a great defensive catcher, and was not up the standards set by Larry Brown, Biz Mackey, and Frank Duncan. But few teams ran on him, and when a man hits .380 with power, there's always a position available.

Right: Josh Gibson never got to play in the Major Leagues, but in 1972 he was rightfully placed among the best who ever played baseball.

Far right: Josh Gibson was the rare batter who combined a great batting eye with tape-measure power.

Gibson's family moved to Pittsburgh when Josh was young, and he began playing against grown men when he was 15. Gibson was playing with the Pittsburgh Crawfords semipro team (not the top team he would later play for) when he was discovered by the Homestead Grays. In 1930, when regular catcher Buck Ewing broke a finger, Gibson took over full time and was a sensation from the start. He led the team to the league championship while batting over .400.

The next year, 1931, the Grays fielded what many think is the greatest team in black baseball history. Gibson was the greatest player of them all, hitting, according to some accounts, 70 homers. The Grays, with Oscar Charleston, Smokey Joe Williams, Double Duty Radcliffe, Jud Wilson, and Willie Foster, among others, won 136 out of 153 games during the season, then beat a Major League All-Star team featuring Lefty Grove, Harry Heilmann, and Heinie Manush (all Hall of Famers), by scores of 10-7 and 18-0, with Gibson leading the way.

The following season, the Pittsburgh Crawfords' Gus Greenlee stole most of the Grays'

stars for his own team, and for a five-year period they were one of the best teams in history, with Gibson and "Satchel" Paige leading the way. During this period, Gibson rolled up his uniform sleeves to expose his bulging biceps, batted over .400, averaged more than 50 homers per season, and, against white semipro teams, was advertised as guaranteeing he would hit a home run every game.

In 1936, the Negro National League sent a team to the Denver Post tournament, one of the top assemblies of baseball talent outside the Majors, and it was during this tournament that Gibson truly showed what separated him from the rest of the great hitters of his day. While his team swept through the tournament in seven straight games, Gibson homered five times and batted over .500. Every time he homered, some would claim it was the farthest blast they'd ever seen.

Gibson went with "Satchel" Paige to the Dominican Republic for the end of the 1937 season along with several other Crawfords, and Greenlee's team was, for all intents and purposes, over as a top team. Dictator Rafael Trujillo was in a tight political spot and he hoped winning the

Above: Josh Gibson (attempting to score) batted close to .500 in East–West games.

Left: Though known primarily for his hitting, Gibson (sliding) could run and throw with the best in the Negro Leagues.

country's baseball pennant would help his re-election hopes. Gibson batted .453 in his stay on the island, and led the league in RBIs, despite missing the first few weeks of the season.

When Gibson returned to the United States, he went back to his baseball roots, signing with the Homestead Grays—it would be the last Negro League team he would play for. Batting after Buck Leonard in the lineup, Gibson would lead the Grays to Negro National League pennants for nine straight seasons (1937–1945).

In 1940 Gibson jumped to the Mexican League with Veracruz and hit .467 with 11 homers in just 22 games.

The Grays had two home fields during Gibson's reign as home run king, the Pittsburgh Pirates' Forbes Field and Washington Senators' Griffith Stadium, and it has been said that most years Gibson hit more homers into the left field bleachers at Griffith Stadium (410 feet down the line) than the entire American League.

According to "Double Duty" Radcliffe, third basemen lived in fear every time Gibson came to the plate. Sam Hairston remembered nearly being killed by a line drive off Gibson's bat despite playing a few steps on the outfield grass.

Unfortunately, Gibson's story has a sad ending. After years of suffering occasional mental breakdowns and severe hypertension, Gibson suffered a fatal stroke in January 1947, a month after turning 35 and less than three months before Jackie Robinson would play for the Brooklyn Dodgers.

Though he never made the Major Leagues, all Negro Leaguers agree that Gibson would have been a Major League superstar, and would have a chapter of the record books all to himself. Besides the National Baseball Hall of Fame in Cooperstown, Gibson is also enshrined in the Mexican and Puerto Rican Baseball Halls of Fame.

Willie Foster

Born: June 12, 1904, in Calvert, TX
Died: September 16, 1978, in Lorman, MS
Inducted into the Hall of Fame: 1996
Position: Pitcher
Batted: both
Threw: left
Height: 6ft 1in
Weight: 200lb
Years: 1922–1938
Teams: Memphis Red Sox, Chicago American Giants, Birmingham Black Barons, Homestead Grays, Kansas City Monarchs, Cole's American Giants, Pittsburgh Crawfords.

The Negro Leagues produced many great left-handed pitchers, but Willie Foster was thought to be the best of them all. "He could have made history if he played in the Major Leagues," stated one player. Foster was similar to Warren Spahn, thought many players; a very stylish lefty with a great fastball, curve, and control.

Foster was the half-brother of black baseball czar Rube Foster, and grew up in Mississippi. After developing his pitching skills at Alcorn College, Foster asked his brother Rube if he could tryout with the American Giants. Rube refused, and the two were never very close afterward. A few years later, though, Rube did call for Willie and he became the ace of the Giants' staff.

In 1926, with Rube in a mental hospital, Willie almost single-handedly carried the American Giants to the Negro National League pennant. During the regular season, Foster won more than 30 games, and in the playoffs against the Kansas City Monarchs, Foster won both ends of a double-header (both against Bullet Rogan) to claim the pennant. In the ensuing World Series against the Atlantic City Bacharachs, Foster won two games.

1927 was a repeat of the year before with Foster again winning 30 games (18-3 in league games) and again winning two games in the World Series against Atlantic City.

Right: Willie Foster, the greatest lefthander in Negro League history.

In 1933, Foster journeyed to North Dakota to play a game with the integrated semipro Jamestown Red Sox. The Red Sox' rivals, the Bismarck Churchills, had hired "Satchel" Paige and Jamestown wanted someone who could beat him. Foster pitched a great game against Bismarck, striking out 10 and allowing only six hits, but one of those hits was a single off the bat of Paige in the ninth that won the game for the capital city.

Word from Chicago came that Paige and Foster had both been voted to oppose each other in the first East-West All-Star game. Paige chose to stay in North Dakota, but Foster returned to Chicago where he pitched a complete game and beat the East squad, 11-7.

In 1934, Paige and Foster did oppose each other in the East-West game, with Paige getting the victory, though Foster gave up only one run. In 1935, Foster finally got his revenge on Paige by beating him in an important game in September. However, his arm was already starting to show the signs of age. After another solid season in 1936, Foster's career in the Negro Leagues was pretty much over.

After retiring, Foster became the baseball coach and dean of men at his alma mater, Alcorn College in Mississippi.

In the famous 1952 *Pittsburgh Courier* poll, Foster was placed on the first team on a pitching staff with "Smokey" Joe Williams, "Satchel" Paige, Bullet Rogan, and John Donaldson.

Monte Irvin

Born: February 25, 1919, in Halesburg, AL
Inducted into the Hall of Fame: 1973
Height: 6ft 1in
Weight: 190lb
Positions: Outfield, third base
Batted: right
Threw: right
Years: 1937–1957
Teams: Newark Eagles, Mexico, New York Giants, Minneapolis Millers, Chicago Cubs.

What might have been? That's the question that comes to mind when discussing Monte Irvin and his baseball career. What if he had been allowed to play in the Major Leagues as a 20-year-old instead of a 30-year-old? What if World War II had not interrupted his career for several years? What if he hadn't been injured just when his Major League career was starting?

Many Negro Leaguers thought Irvin would have been the obvious choice to integrate the Majors instead of Jackie Robinson, because Irvin could do absolutely everything on a baseball field. He hit for power and average, had great speed, a great arm, and a great baseball mind.

Irvin was born in Alabama, but grew up in New Jersey and earned 16 letters in four sports at East Orange High School. He then attended Lincoln College, while playing for the Newark Eagles on weekends under the name "Jimmy Nelson" to keep his amateur status.

Irvin led the Negro National League in batting twice with averages close to .400 and, along with Willie Wells, Leon Day, Larry Doby, and Mule Suttles, made the Eagles one of the top teams in the Negro National League throughout the late 1930s and 1940s.

Below: Monte Irvin was considered the top Major League prospect in the 1940s before he was drafted into the Army.

Irvin won the batting title and home run crown in Mexico in 1942, and, at the time, might have been the greatest player not in the Major Leagues. When Irvin returned to the United States in 1943 he was drafted into the army and missed the next three seasons. Although he returned to baseball in 1945, he never quite regained the skills he had previously shown in 1942.

In the winter of 1945–46, Irvin won the Puerto Rican League Most Valuable Player award, leading San Juan to the championship. Upon returning to the United States, he helped the Newark Eagles win the Negro League World Series in 1946 over the Kansas City Monarchs, batting .462 with three homers.

Irvin played in six East-West All-Star games with the Eagles, his last in 1948. In 1949, Irvin was signed by the New York Giants and assigned to the Jersey City Giants in the Minors where he batted .373. In July, he and Hank Thompson were called up for a cup of coffee and became the first blacks to play for the Giants.

The next year he again started in Jersey City, but was called up to the Giants after batting over .500 with 10 homers in the first two weeks of the Minor League season. He batted .299 for the 1950 season, then became a star in 1951, leading the National League in RBIs (121) while batting .312, blasting 24 homers, and stealing 12 bases in 14 attempts. He also batted over .450 in the World Series, but the Giants lost to the Yankees.

Early in the 1952 season, Irvin broke his ankle sliding into third and his career was downhill from there. 1953 was Irvin's last good season, batting .329 with 21 homers and 97 RBIs; he wouldn't bat .300 or hit 20 homers again. After a modest season with the Chicago Cubs in 1956, and a couple games in the Pacific Coast League, Irvin was done as a player at age 38.

Irvin ended his Major League career with a .293 average and 99 homers. These were appropriate numbers for the unlucky Irvin: not quite .300 and not quite 100 homers. But who knows what might have been?

In the famous 1952 *Pittsburgh Courier* poll, Irvin was named to the starting outfield with Oscar Charleston and Cristobel Torriente. Besides the National Baseball Hall of Fame in Cooperstown, New York, Irvin was also inducted into the Mexican and Cuban Baseball Halls of Fame.

William Judy Johnson

Born: October 26, 1899, in Snow Hill, MD
Died: June 15, 1989, in Wilmington, DE
Inducted into the Hall of Fame: 1975
Positions: Third base
Batted: right
Threw: right
Height: 5ft 11in
Weight: 145lb
Years: 1918–1937
Teams: Atlantic City Bacharachs, Madison Stars, Hilldale Daisies, Homestead Grays, Pittsburgh Crawfords.

If you look strictly at batting statistics, you may wonder why Judy Johnson, with good but not great numbers, is enshrined in the Hall of Fame. His value to a team, though, belied mere numbers.

First, Johnson was one of the great clutch hitters of his era, making each hit count. Second, he had one of the game's greatest minds, always studying the game and his opponents to gain every advantage he could. Third, he played one of the slickest third bases ever.

He has been compared defensively to Brooks Robinson and most think his arm was much stronger. He came in on bunts, cut off balls in the hole, and stabbed balls down the line. If he had used the bigger gloves of Robinson's day, he might never have missed a grounder!

Johnson grew up in Wilmington, Delaware, and played baseball for his dad's Royal Blues as a teenager. Johnson quit high school and worked on the docks in New Jersey through World War I, before signing with the Madison Wisconsin Stars, the equivalent of a Minor League black team. It was with the Stars that Johnson picked up the nickname "Judy" because he resembled teammate Judy Gans.

In 1920, Judy made the black big time when he was discovered and signed by the Philadelphia Hilldales. For several years, Johnson teamed with Jake Stevens as black baseball's best left-side infield pair. As a hitter, Johnson was the man teams hated to see at the plate because he would do anything to get on base. If he couldn't hit a certain pitcher, then he'd lean into a pitch, take a walk, anything. He was a team player all the way.

In his prime, Johnson batted as high as .380 with moderate power and around 20 stolen bases. However as he got older, he became more of a .280 hitter. He knew his job was to get on base for the big hitters, and he never tried to do any more than that. Off the field, Johnson is remembered as having a sweet personality, consistent with his nickname of "Mr. Sunshine."

In the first modern Negro League World Series in 1924, Johnson led the Hilldales with a .341 average including a game winning home run, but the Kansas City Monarchs won the series five games to four. In 1925, the same teams met again

Far left: Judy Johnson was valuable in ways that couldn't always be measured in statistics.

Right: Despite playing with the likes of Josh Gibson, Jud Wilson, and Oscar Charleston, it was Johnson that opposing pitchers hated to see at the plate.

in the World Series with the Hilldales winning and becoming the only Eastern Colored League team to ever win the Championship. Johnson may have only batted only .250, but, as usual, his few hits were very important.

Johnson was named the East's best third baseman in 1925 in a poll taken by the *Pittburgh Courier*, and the most valuable player in the East in 1929 by *Courier* sports editor Rollo Wilson.

After leaving the Hilldales, Johnson spent some of his best seasons with the Crawfords where he batted well over .300 every year from 1932–1936.

In a 1952 *Courier* poll, Johnson was named the second best third baseman in Negro League history, behind only Oliver Marcelle. After retiring as a player, Johnson became a Major League scout with several teams including the Milwaukee Braves, for which he discovered Bill Bruton, his future son-in-law.

Unlike many Negro Leaguers, Johnson was able to enjoy his Hall of Fame inclusion as he lived for 14 years after his induction before dying at the age of 88.

Right: "Was Buck Leonard a great clutch hitter?" laughed "Double Duty" Radcliffe. "Great 'all-kinda' hitter!"

Below: Buck Leonard in a rare moment of relaxation. Leonard's Homestead Grays were often the most traveled team in the World!

Walter Fennar "Buck" Leonard

Born: September 8, 1907, in Rocky Mount, North Carolina
Died: November 27, 1997, Rocky Mount, North Carolina
Inducted into the Hall of Fame: 1972
Batted: left
Threw: left
Height: 5ft 11in
Weight: 190lb
Years: 1933–1953
Teams: Brooklyn Royal Giants, Homestead Grays, Mexico.

"You couldn't get a fastball by him if you shot it with a cannon!" was how one Negro Leaguer described pitching to "Buck" Leonard, one of the greatest all-around hitters in baseball history. Though not a huge man, Leonard hit the ball harder and farther than any batter this side of Josh Gibson, which adds credence to the theory that he was "the Black Lou Gehrig." Gibson, like Babe Ruth, got most of the headlines, but Leonard quietly and consistently hit in the .350 range and usually belted 30-40 homers per season.

He was born and died in Rocky Mount, North Carolina, and in the 85 years in-between he made life miserable for pitchers, played the smoothest

first base in the Negro Leagues, and earned the title as one of baseball's classiest gentlemen.

Leonard was groomed into a great first baseman by old-timer Ben Taylor of the famous Negro League Taylor brothers while playing with a semipro team out of Baltimore in 1933. Taylor, past his prime, groomed Leonard to replace him, but he ended up leaving for the Brooklyn Royal Giants in late 1933, managed by "Cannonball" Dick Redding. The next season Leonard, by a recommendation from "Smokey" Joe Williams, was signed by the Grays and he stayed with them until the team folded in 1950.

It was not uncommon on Negro League teams for the first baseman to play the role of the clown, catching balls with one hand, or behind their backs during warm-ups. Leonard, however, was strictly business on the field.

From 1937-1945, Leonard held down first base for the Homestead Grays as they won nine straight Negro National League pennants. Leonard played in 13 East-West games, batting .313 and hitting homers off Theolic Smith, "Double Duty" Radcliffe, and Ted Trent. In all, Leonard played in more All-Star games, had more homers, more RBIs, and more total bases than any other player. Leonard played several years in Mexico, Puerto Rico, Venezuela, and Cuba, and everywhere he traveled he hit, averaging well over a .300 average with power in foreign countries.

In 1948, Leonard led the Negro National League in batting with a .385 average, and tied for the league lead in homers. At the end of the season, Leonard's Grays beat the Birmingham Black Barons and 17-year-old Willie Mays, for the last Negro League World Series title—according to Leonard, his biggest baseball thrill. In 1955, at age 48, he batted over .300 with 13 homers in 62 games in the Central Mexican League in the Minors.

Homestead Grays owner Cum Posey listed Leonard as the top first baseman he ever saw. "Double Duty" Radcliffe, a player and manager for 40 years, said Leonard, over all others, was the man he'd want in the batter's box with a game on the line. "Was he a great clutch hitter?" remarked Radcliffe. "He was a great 'all kind of' hitter!"

In Negro League play, Leonard's lifetime average was close to .340, and against all competition

was near .400. He hit home runs at a clip that would have averaged 35–40 in a full Major League season. In exhibitions he batted over .400 versus Major Leaguers. Anyway you slice it, Buck Leonard could hit!

John Henry "Pop" Lloyd

Born: April 25, 1884, in Palatka, FL
Died: March 19, 1965, in Atlantic City, NJ
Inducted into the Hall of Fame: 1976
Position: Shortstop, first base
Batted: left
Threw: right
Height: 6ft
Weight: 180lb
Years: 1906–1931
Teams: Macon Acmes, Cuban X-Giants, Philadelphia Giants, Chicago Lelands, New York Lincolns, Chicago American Giants, Brooklyn Royal Giants, Atlantic City Bacharachs, Columbus Buckeyes, Hilldale Daisies, Harlem Stars

John Henry "Pop" Lloyd was the Alex Rodriguez of his day—a large shortstop who could hit. Although several inches shorter than "A-Rod" and Cal Ripken, Jr., Lloyd was a large shortstop for his era, and only the Kansas City Monarchs' Dobie Moore could hit with him among middle infielders.

Lloyd was discovered by Rube Foster in 1905 when Foster's Cuban X-Giants passed through Jacksonville, Florida. The next season the X-Giants sent for Lloyd and over the next two decades he played with some of the greatest teams of the era, usually whichever one offered him the most money.

By 1911, Lloyd was the top shortstop in black baseball and a .400 hitter. In 1913, Lloyd was player-manager of the New York Lincoln Giants and he led them to a tremendous record, and a thrashing of Rube Foster's American Giants in a series for the championship. Foster couldn't lick 'em, so he asked Lloyd to join his team, and Lloyd was an American Giant for several seasons.

Lloyd played for several teams after Chicago, before spending most of his last great years with the Atlantic City Bacharachs. In 1924, Lloyd switched to second base in deference to shortstop Dick Lundy, just as black baseball's first big shortstop,

Left: John Henry "Pop" Lloyd, the first power-hitting shortstop in black baseball history.

"Homerun" Johnson, had done for Lloyd on the Lincoln Giants in 1913. Lloyd took to the new position and he led the league in batting.

Lloyd played some of his best ball in Cuba where he was nicknamed "the shovel" for the way he scooped up a glove-full of dirt with the ball before firing the ball to first, much like the Majors' Honus Wagner.

Lloyd played semipro ball until he was almost 60, ending with the Farley Stars in Atlantic City. He then became a grade school janitor where he spun tales of his playing days and was loved by children until the day he died.

One baseball writer who covered Major League games as well as black baseball said that Lloyd, and not Ruth, was the best player in all of baseball. Connie Mack also said he was the best player he'd ever seen.

Available statistics show Lloyd batting close to .350 lifetime and leading the league in stolen bases and home runs several times.

Wilbur ("Bullet" Joe) Rogan

Born: July 28, 1889, in Oklahoma City, OK
Died: March 4, 1967, in Kansas City, MO
Inducted into the Hall of Fame: 1988
Positions: Pitcher, outfield (also manager and umpire)
Batted: right
Threw: right
Height: 5ft 7in
Weight: 190lb
Years: 1917–1938
Teams: Kansas City Monarchs, All-Nations

When the most versatile players in Negro League history are discussed, the names brought up most often are Martin Dihigo and "Bullet" Joe Rogan. They couldn't have looked more different from each other and been so similar in their talents. Dihigo was a huge, handsome Cuban who was a great pitcher and one of the league's best outfielders... *continued on page 161*

THE GREATS

Leroy "Satchel" Paige

Born: July 7, 1900 or 1906, in Mobile, AL
Died: June 8, 1982, in Kansas City, MO
Inducted into the Hall of Fame: 1971
Position: Pitcher
Batted: right
Threw: right
Height: 6ft 4in
Weight: 180lb
Years: 1924–1967
Teams (partial list): Birmingham Black Barons, Cleveland Cubs, Pittsburgh Crawfords, Kansas City Monarchs, Bismarck Churchills, Ciudad Trujillo (Dominican Republic), Chicago American Giants, Memphis Red Sox, Cleveland Indians, Portland

Beavers, Kansas City Athletics, St. Louis Browns. So much has been written about Satchel Paige, some truth and some pure legend, that it is difficult to write a brief summary of his career.

He most certainly grew up in Mobile, Alabama, in the early years of the 20th century, and quickly became a good pitcher. The genesis of his nickname "Satchel" has many versions, but the most likely is that he stole satchels from the local train station when he was a kid. Not long after receiving the name, Satchel was in reform school, where he stayed until he was 18. It was in reform school that Paige polished his pitching skills.

Paige didn't, however, become dominant overnight. When Paige joined his first top-flight Negro League team, the 1927 Birmingham Black Barons, he was far from their best pitcher. The Barons had Robert Poindexter, Harry Salmon, and "Steel Arm" Dickey ahead of him, but Paige was a quick study.

By 1930, Paige had filled out a little which made his fastball overwhelming, had worked tirelessly on his control, and had a personality like no other. These, and the fact that he had the unusual ability to pitch almost every day without hurting his arm, made him the top gate attraction in black baseball history. Every town in the country was willing to pay to see this tall, gangly black man strike out the greatest sluggers they could offer.

No man ever threw a faster fastball than Paige. "Overbearing!" described catcher "Double Duty" Radcliffe. "You have fastballs," recalled former Atlanta Black Cracker Norman Lumpkin. "You have faster balls, you have some lightening balls, you have some peas, and you have some pitchers like Satchel that you'd rather not even face."

From 1930 until 1938, Paige pitched thousands of innings for whatever team would pay his going rate and he rarely lost. In 1935, playing for an integrated team in Bismarck, North Dakota, Paige

Left: "This face has seen some sights, it and me," remarked Satchel Paige in his latter years.

Right: Was Satchel Paige nervous about playing for brutal Dominican dictator Rafael Trujillo in 1937? Notice how he buttoned his shirt!

pitched in more than 60 games in three months, won 30 of 32 decisions, and averaged almost 15 strikeouts per game.

Paige was the ace of the Pittsburgh Crawfords during the 1930s winning about 30 games a year, and pitching relief in almost every other game as he was advertised to do so.

"Satchel just didn't make mistakes," explained Negro Leaguer Sherwood Brewer. "If you told him, 'Satch, this guy likes fastballs,' he'd say, 'Well, where does he like his fastballs?' If he threw a pitch outside, that's where he wanted to throw it!"

In 1937, Paige left the Crawfords and played a month in the Dominican Republic for president Rafael Trujillo. He went 8-2 for the Ciudad Trujillo

Dragons and won the championship game against Chet Brewer and the Aguilas Cibaenas team when teammate Sammy Bankhead hit a grand slam.

In 1938, the innings caught up with Satchel and his arm went dead. Today, maybe he would have had surgery and been back in a year, but back in the 1930s the only advice given was rest. Most thought he was washed up

His name still drew crowds, though, so he was signed by Kansas City Monarchs owner J.L. Wilkinson to play on the Monarchs "B" team. Paige would throw a few innings with not much on the ball and play first base; that was good enough for most fans in small towns to feel they got their money's worth.

Miraculously, in 1939, his arm recovered and a new generation of sluggers got the privilege of striking out against the master. He used a variety of windups and deliveries, but he was still mainly a fastball pitcher with unrivaled control.

Through the 1940s Paige helped the Monarchs to five Negro American League pennants and the World Series championship in 1942.

For most of the 1930s and 1940s, Paige put together an All-Star team to play on the West Coast in Autumn against Big Leaguers; first Dizzy Dean's All-Stars, then Bob Feller's All-Stars. When historians try to figure out why Negro League teams beat Major League teams so often in barnstorming games, the answer could be as simple as the name "Satchel" Paige.

Paige was almost as famous for his team-jumping as he was for his pitching. God only knows how many teams he pitched for over the years but it was several hundred at least.

Negro Leaguers were somewhat mixed on their feelings for Satchel. Some were jealous of the money he made and the fact that he played by his own rules. Some didn't like that he couldn't always be counted on to show up to games he was supposed to. But most agree that he was a hell of a lot of fun to be around, that if he showed up you could

Left: Fashions came and went, but Satchel Paige kept striking batters out!

Above: Cleveland Indians manager Lou Boudreau (left) with Satchel Paige and Bob Feller, two pitchers who barnstormed against each other for years.

count on a win, and that his popularity helped keep Negro League baseball alive during its lean years, like Babe Ruth kept the Majors alive. If a Negro League team was having money problems, they'd send for Paige and he would draw enough fans in one game to keep teams going for another few months.

Paige did finally make the Majors in 1948 with the Cleveland Indians and went 6-1, helped the Cleveland Indians win the pennant, and, most importantly to owner Bill Veeck, packed the house every time he pitched.

Veeck kept buying teams over the next decade and Paige followed to the St. Louis Browns, Portland Beavers, and Miami Beach Flamingos. In-between Paige barnstormed with his own All-Star team, logging more miles than an over-the-road trucker.

Dr. Bob Price was a young slugger in the Dixie League in Paducah, Kentucky, in 1959 when he faced Paige and his barnstorming team. "The umpire called me out and I never heard such an ovation for striking out," he recalled. "I remember riding home in the truck with my Dad and him saying, 'Son I'm proud of you. You were struck out by the great Satchel Paige.'"

Paige's last appearance in a Big League game came in 1965 when he pitched three shutout innings for the Kansas City Athletics. The only hit he gave up was a double to the Red Sox's Carl Yastrzemski.

Paige pitched more games that any man in history, in almost every town in North America, and won well over 1000 games. When he was in his prime, it was not unusual for Paige to not allow a ball to reach the outfield.

A field in his adopted home town of Kansas City was named after him, and a few weeks after attending the naming ceremony Paige was dead at age 76 (or 82). "I've said it once and I'll say it a hundred times," Paige often said, "I'm forty-four years-old."

In 1971 Paige was inducted into the National Baseball Hall of Fame in Cooperstown. In 1996 he was inducted into the Puerto Rican Baseball Hall of Fame.

THE GREATS

Jackie Robinson

Born: January 31, 1919, in Cairo, GA
Died: October 24, 1972, in Stamford, CT
Inducted into the Hall of Fame: 1962
Positions: Shortstop, second base, first base, third base, outfield
Batted: right
Threw: right
Height: 5ft 11in
Weight: 200lb
Teams: Kansas City Monarchs, Montreal Royals, Brooklyn Dodgers.

Under normal circumstances, a muscle-bound infielder with an average arm and only one season

of Negro League experience would not be the perfect candidate to integrate Organized Baseball. This was the resumé that Jackie Robinson carried, though, when he was scouted by Brooklyn Dodger president Branch Rickey and scout Clyde Sukeforth.

Negro League players, as a group, agreed that Robinson wasn't the best player in the league when he was chosen in 1945. There were other players who were considered "can't misses" talent-wise such as Monte Irvin, Piper Davis, Artie Wilson, Larry Doby, Avelino Canizares, or Leon Day—even "Satchel" Paige, at his advanced age. But, to Branch Rickey's credit, he and his scouts saw something in Robinson that was special. It was Robinson's fire and an incredible will to succeed, more than his baseball skills, in Rickey's mind, that made him a "can't miss." Also, his experience as an officer in the Army and his history of playing sports with whites rounded out his candidacy.

Robinson was built like a football player, which is understandable since it was on the UCLA football field that he had achieved his most athletic success. He was also a letter winner in baseball, track, and basketball. In fact, many believe baseball was Robinson's fourth best sport, or maybe fifth if you consider his immense talent in golf.

Robinson had good power for a middle infielder, was an outstanding base runner, had a solid glove, but only a mediocre throwing arm. His throwing arm is what had many Negro League veterans worried. "If he doesn't make it," they argued, "how long will we have to wait for another player to get a chance?"

In his short stay in the Negro Leagues with the Kansas City Monarchs, he batted over .300 and was tutored on the finer points of the game by Negro League veterans such as Jesse Williams, Hilton Smith, Frank Duncan, Bonnie Serrell, and "Double Duty" Radcliffe. These players learned from Robinson about a new generation of black men who weren't

Left: Jackie Robinson signs his Brooklyn Dodger contract with Branch Rickey looking on. Rickey's "experiment" changed America.

Right: Jackie Robinson, the first black Major Leaguer of the modern era.

simply willing to "go along to get along." Robinson wanted to make changes immediately.

Many Monarchs remembered an incident at a gas station in the South when Robinson opened their collective eyes. The gas station, as was their policy for as long as the Monarchs could remember, let the team purchase gas, but its rest rooms were off limits. Robinson, the rookie on the team, confronted the gas station owner and gave him an ultimatum: either we can use the rest rooms or we don't buy your gas! The owner relented, realizing that the hundreds of gallons of gas he sold to black teams were at stake. The older players couldn't help wondering to themselves, "Why didn't we do that sooner?" While Negro Leaguers of an earlier generation still had the attitude that they shouldn't rock the boat, Robinson let the world know that he wouldn't put up with a single injustice.

Of course attitude and leadership skills can carry a player only so far. The fact was that Robinson could flat-out play baseball. Rickey

signed him and assigned him to the Montreal Royals of the International League in 1946; Robinson switched to second base and tore up the league. In his first game, Robinson singled three times, homered, stole two bases, and scored four runs. Despite death threats, harsh fans on the road, and a near-nervous breakdown, Robinson lead the league in hitting (.349), stolen bases (49), and fielding average (.985) to go with 113 runs, 25 doubles, and 66 RBIs. For good measure, he led his team to the pennant and a win in the Little World Series against the Louisville Red Birds of the American Association.

In 1947, Robinson joined the Dodgers and continued his outstanding play by batting .297, leading the league in stolen bases (29), winning Rookie of the Year honors and leading the Dodgers to the World Series. Robinson almost single-handedly managed to bring the stolen base and bunt back to Major League baseball after a long layoff. Instead of grabbing the bat at the end of the handle

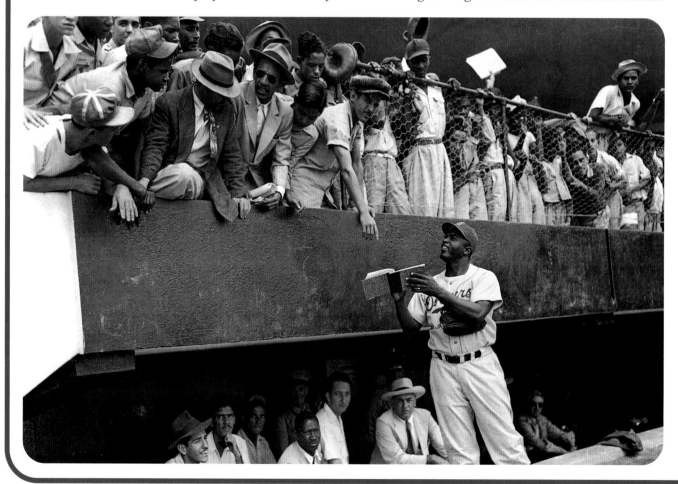

and swinging from the heels, Robinson used bunting, speed, aggressive base-running, and the element of fear in order to dominate the game. For years the game had been played "by the book," but Robinson used different methods and played by instinct, brains, and daring—Negro League baseball in a nutshell.

Negro Leaguer Maurice Peatros stated it well when he said, "We didn't give a damn about the score. If you could steal third base, you stole third base! Damn the score! They talk now about 'running up the score'—well if we could score 20, we scored 20!"

Many people hear the name Jackie Robinson and think about stealing home, which he did 20 times. It further emphasizes Robinson's attitude that he wasn't going to wait for someone else to do something for him. He wanted it right now, whether it was a run, or the right to use a rest room.

In 1949 Robinson was the best player in baseball, winning the Most Valuable player award, winning the batting title (.342), leading the league in stolen bases (37), belting 16 homers, and driving in 124 runs.

Robinson moved to third base and eventually to left field as he got older, and in 1955 the Brooklyn Dodgers won their only World Series, against the New York Yankees. The Dodgers made the World Series again in 1956, but lost to the Yankees. That winter, Robinson was traded to the New York Giants, the hated rivals of the Dodgers; Robinson retired instead of playing for his arch enemies, and five years later he was in the Hall of Fame. His lifetime batting average was .311. He continued to fight for equality until the day he died, prematurely at age 53.

Below left: Though visiting fans often treated Robinson terribly, in Brooklyn's Ebbets Field, he was a hero.

Below: Jackie Robinson played with a burning desire to win every game.

and second baseman. Rogan, who was built like a miniature Babe Ruth—short and stocky with skinny legs—was also a great pitcher who could bat cleanup and play center field when he wasn't on the mound. Both Dihigo and Rogan also had the immense confidence that came with such extraordinary talent.

Negro League star Bobby Robinson classed Rogan with "Satchel" Paige and Carl Glass as the best pitchers he ever faced, and teammate Will Owen thought Rogan was the toughest of them all.

Rogan threw hard, with a sharp curve and "inshoot"—what we now call a slider. He usually pitched without a windup, like Don Larsen would years later.

Rogan is most associated with the Kansas City Monarchs, a team he played for from 1920–1938, from age 30 to 47. Prior to joining the Monarchs,

Rogan played with the famous 15th Infantry team at Fort Huachua where he drew the attention of Casey Stengel, who recommended him to the Monarchs owner, J.L. Wilkinson.

Rogan was in his pitching prime in the early 1920s, and old-timers insist he was every bit as fast as "Satchel" Paige. Many others say he would also have been their choice to pitch a big game because his great hitting added so much to his value as a pitcher.

In 1921, Rogan faced and beat a barnstorming team led by Babe Ruth, and in the first Negro League World Series in 1924, Rogan batted .325 with two wins to lead the Monarchs to the championship. Rogan became player-manager of the Monarchs in 1926 and he was a hard-driving manager in the mold of Billy Martin. In the 1927 Negro National League playoffs, Rogan let his ego get the best of him when he pitched himself in both ends of a doubleheader and lost both games to Willie Foster.

Rogan played several winters in California during the 1920s and 1930s. In 1929 he led the Philadelphia Royal Giants to the league

Left: "Bullet" Joe Rogan won games with his booming bat and pitching arm.

Below: After his playing days were over, Rogan (left) became a Negro League umpire.

championship against teams loaded with Major League stars such as Jimmie Foxx, Al Simmons, Earl Averill, and Smead Jolley.

An account of a doubleheader between the Monarchs and a top white semipro team emphasized Rogan's versatility: "In center field he made a great catch and a greater throw to first for a double play, at short he made a marvelous one-handed, cross-arm catch which brought great applause from the stands. His pitching was so deceptive that [the opposing team] could hardly see the ball." He also homered in both games.

In 1936, at age 47, Rogan made his only East-West All-Star appearance, then spent his final years with the Monarchs when they were mostly a traveling team.

Most seasons, Rogan could be counted on to win 75 percent of his mound decisions, and bat anywhere from .330-.400. After retiring from playing, Rogan stayed in baseball as a manager and umpire. Rogan, along with Dihigo and "Double Duty" Radcliffe, probably won more than 300 games on the mound while blasting 300 home runs. No wonder he was confident.

Hilton Smith

Born: February 27, 1912, in Giddings, TX
Died: November 18, 1983, in Kansas City, MO
Inducted into the Hall of Fame: 2001
Batted: right
Threw: right
Height: 6ft 2in
Weight: 180lb
Years: 1932–1950
Teams: Kansas City Monarchs, Monroe Monarchs, Bismarck Churchills, Fulda Giants.

One of the best pitchers you might not know anything about was Hilton Smith. He had it all: speed, control, a great curveball, and intelligence. The reason you may not know much about Smith is because, for most of his career, he played in the enormous shadow of "Satchel" Paige. Negro Leaguers generally agree, though, that Smith was Paige's superior in the late 1930s and early 1940s.

Smith grew up in Texas and played for the Austin Black Senators before joining the Monroe

Monarchs in 1932 which featured great pitcher Barney Morris, outfielder Red Parnell, and Augustus Sanders.

Monroe won the Southern League pennant and Smith got a chance to see how he stacked up against top Negro Leaguers when his Monarchs played the Pittsburgh Crawfords in a roving "World Series." Smith lost his only start against the star-studded Craws, but he was just coming into his prime.

After a few seasons in Monroe, Smith signed with the Bismarck, North Dakota integrated team in 1935 joining a pitching staff that featured Barney Morris, "Double Duty" Radcliffe, Chet Brewer, and "Satchel" Paige. Paige got all the headlines, but Smith went 6 and 1, and batted .343. Bismarck entered and won the first national semipro championship in Wichita, Kansas, but Smith didn't pitch a single inning. When a teammate was too hung over to play in the championship game, however, Smith played right field, batted clean up, and went 2 for 4, boosting his average for the tournament to .444 and helped Bismarck become National Champions. Smith was an outstanding hitter with power, and at least one Negro Leaguer thought that he could have played in any outfield in baseball because of his potent bat.

In 1936, Smith returned to Bismarck and Paige didn't. It might have been the best thing that could have happened to Smith as he assumed the role as the team's top pitcher. He was every bit as impressive as Paige had been the year before. At the end of the season, Bismarck returned to Wichita to defend their title, and although they came up short, Smith won four games: a two-hit shutout, a three-hit shutout, a 10-1 win, and a win in 6-⅓ innings of relief.

After the tournament, Hilton Smith signed with the Kansas City Monarchs, and he stayed with them until 1948. In the ten-year period from 1937 through 1946, Smith may have been the best pitcher in baseball—arguments could be made for Leon Day and Bob Feller—as he won at least 20 every season.

Smith pitched in the East-West game seven times, winning one decision and losing two. After his arm started bothering him in 1948 he signed to play integrated baseball again, this time with the

Left: Hilton Smith was Satchel Paige's equal on the mound, but his shy personality kept him out of the headlines.

Fulda, Minnesota Giants. By this time, Smith was using several illegal pitches he had learned from former teammate "Double Duty" Radcliffe to get by, and he did well.

In games against Major Leaguers, Smith won six of his seven decisions, including a one-hitter versus the New York Yankees in 1947. That same year, Smith was offered a contract with the Brooklyn Dodgers, but at age 35 he knew he didn't have much left. In league games only, Smith is credited with 161 wins and only 32 losses, a winning percentage of .834.

In the early 1980s, Smith stepped out of character as a modest man, and wrote to the Hall of Fame asking for them to consider his fine record. Twenty years later, long after Smith had passed away, he was inducted into Cooperstown in 2001.

Norman "Turkey" Stearnes

Born: May 8, 1901, in Nashville, TN
Died: September 4, 1979, in Detroit, MI
Inducted into the Hall of Fame: 2000
Batted: left
Threw: left
Height: 6ft
Weight: 170lb
Years: 1923–1945
Teams: Nashville Elite Giants, Montgomery Grey Sox, Memphis Red Sox, Detroit Stars, New York Lincolns, Kansas City Monarchs, Cole's American Giants, Chicago American Giants, Philadelphia Stars, Detroit Black Sox, Toledo Cubs.

Next to Josh Gibson, "Turkey" Stearnes may have been the greatest home run hitter the Negro Leagues ever produced. From 1923–1943, Stearnes averaged close to 40 home runs a season, with lifetime totals challenging Hank Aaron's record of 755.

He was born in Nashville, Tennessee, in 1901 and began his career in the Negro Southern League, then considered a Minor League circuit. In 1923, Stearnes joined the Detroit Stars, and played

Above: Norman "Turkey" Stearnes, the Negro League's greatest left-handed power hitter.

It wasn't just the number of homers Stearnes hit that made him special, though. Although he weighed barely 170 pounds, Stearnes talked to his bats and used a Musial-like stance to hit homers great distances, rivaling any by Babe Ruth or Josh Gibson.

"Oh, Turkey broke the record in Detroit," recalled teammate "Double Duty" Radcliffe. "550 feet over the centerfield fence!"

Stearnes could also field with any center fielder in the Negro Leagues, and several players judged him to be the superior of Cool Papa Bell. "Nobody could play more outfield than Turkey," said one player.

Stearnes spent most of his prime winters in the California Winter League, and there he demolished Major League pitching. During the 1928–29 winter, Stearnes joined John Beckwith, Joe Rogan, Biz Mackey, and Rap Dixon on the Cleveland Giants, and won the league championship. In one game he belted three homers.

In 1932, Stearnes joined the Chicago American Giants and not only won the league's triple crown (average, homers, RBIs) but also paced the league in stolen bases. Stearnes, though a quiet unassuming man off the field, was known as a "nasty slider," and would try to punish catchers who stood in the way of him scoring.

In 1933, Stearnes received the most votes of any outfielder for the first East-West All-Star game. He batted leadoff in the game and collected two hits. He would play in four more classics.

In 1934, Stearnes and his Kansas City Monarchs entered the Denver Post semipro tournament and faced the House of David, who had hired "Satchel" Paige, in the championship. Paige beat the Monarchs' Chet Brewer, 2-1, but Stearnes belted a long double off Paige, and made what was called "the greatest play of the tournament" when he hurled himself into a crowd of people who were hanging over the centerfield fence, robbing the batter of a home run. Stearnes batted over .400 for the tournament.

Stearnes retired from the Negro Leagues after playing with the Kansas City Monarchs from 1938–1941. He returned to Detroit where he would live out the rest of his life.

more games with the Stars than any other player. In *Turkey Stearnes and the Detroit Stars* by Richard Bak, Stearnes holds virtually every batting record in Detroit Stars history. In 585 games, Stearnes batted over .350, with 140 homers and won six league home run titles. Using his lifetime home runs per 100 at bats ration, he would have averaged about 40 homers in a modern Major League season.

Willie Wells

Born: August 10, 1905, in Austin, TX
Died: January 22, 1989, in Austin, TX
Inducted into the Hall of Fame: 1997
Positions: Shortstop
Batted: right
Threw: right
Height: 5ft 7in
Weight: 165lb
Years: 1924–1954
Teams: St. Louis Stars, Detroit Wolves, Homestead Grays, Chicago American Giants, Kansas City Monarchs, Newark Eagles, New York Black Yankees, Memphis Red Sox, Birmingham Black Barons, Indianapolis Clowns, Winnipeg Buffaloes.

Willie Wells was simply the greatest all-around shortstop in Negro League history. He was a great fielder, a daring base runner, and a powerful hitter who batted in the heart of the strongest lineups in black baseball. "Double Duty" Radcliffe thought Wells was the best Negro League player, period. "He was such a great shortstop that the ball never hopped bad!" recalled Radcliffe.

Wells batted third for the St. Louis Stars, and because Mule Suttles batted behind him, he got plenty of pitches to hit. And hit he did.

Wells grew up in Texas and played pro ball with the San Antonio Black Aces. In 1924, Wells joined the St. Louis Stars and became an immediate star. The Stars played at Dick Kent's Ballpark, which had a short leftfield fence adjacent to tin car barns. Wells learned to pull the ball, and although he weighed 160 lb dripping wet, he became one of the top home run hitters in baseball. In 1927, Wells set the all-time Negro League record for home runs in one season with 27 in 88 league games.

The Stars won the Negro National League pennant in 1928, 1929, and 1930 with Wells leading a team that included "Cool Papa" Bell, Radcliffe, Roosevelt Davis, and Ted Trent. Wells batted in the .350 range lifetime, but it was against Major Leaguers that he really shined.

Right: Willie "Devil" Wells, the best all-around shortstop in Negro League history.

In 1929, a Negro League All-Star team, featuring Wells, Radcliffe, Willie Foster, Bell, Suttles, Huck Rile, and "Submarine" McDonald whipped the Homestead Grays in a three game series, allowing only one run total.

They then took on a great Major League team featuring Hall of Famers Jimmie Foxx, Heinie Manush, and Charlie Gehringer. In game one, Wells stole home in the ninth to win the game. The Negro Leaguers won game two when Wells singled, tripled twice, and again stole home. The Negro Leaguers won the third game when Wells collected three hits, including the game-winning RBI, and the Major Leaguers finally won the finale, 1-0. In 25 games versus Major Leaguers, Wells batted close to .400.

In 1932, Wells joined the Detroit Wolves, owned by Cum Posey, and also played part of the season with Posey's other team, the Homestead Grays. The Grays played such a hectic schedule that Wells quit the team, claiming his health was in jeopardy if he stayed with them. He played most of the depression years with the Chicago American Giants and Kansas City Monarchs when they were both pretty much barnstorming teams.

Wells was chosen as the shortstop in the first East-West All-Star game in 1933 and contributed two hits to the West's victory. Wells played in a total of eight East-West games, batting .281.

In 1936, Wells joined the Newark Eagles and became part of the famous "Million Dollar Infield" of Wells, third baseman Ray Dandridge, second baseman Dick Seay, and first baseman Mule Suttles. The million dollars represented the infield's collective value to a Major League team, not their salaries.

In 1940, Wells joined many other Negro Leaguers in jumping to Mexico, and he batted close to .350 for the Veracruz Blues. Because black players were treated equal to whites in Mexico, Wells later recalled his years in Mexico as some of his most enjoyable.

In the late 1940s, Wells, back from Mexico, played with the Memphis Red Sox with his son, Willie, Jr.—one of a few father-son duos in Negro League history (Frank Duncan and his son Frank, Jr. and Oliver Marcelle and son Ziggy were two others).

Wells became the player-manager of the Winnipeg Buffaloes in the early 1950s and actually caught several games and hit .300.

In the famous 1952 *Pittsburgh Courier* poll, Wells was edged out by "Pop" Lloyd as the greatest shortstop in Negro League history.

Smokey Joe Williams

Born: April 6, 1885, in Seguin, TX
Died: March 12, 1946, in New York City
Inducted into the Hall of Fame: 1999
Position: Pitcher
Batted: right
Threw: right
Height: 6ft 4in
Weight: 200lb
Years: 1905–1932
Teams: San Antonio Black Broncos, Chicago Giants, New York Lincolns, Mohawk Giants, Chicago American Giants, Atlantic City Bacharachs, Hilldale Daisies, Homestead Grays, Detroit Wolves.

"When I was growing up," remembered Negro Leaguer Josh Johnson, "everyone wanted to be Joe Williams on the sandlot. We argued about who could 'be' Smokey Joe!"

What "Satchel" Paige was to fans in the 1930s and 1940s, Joe Williams was in the 1910s and 1920s. Williams was 6 feet 5 inches when six feet was considered tall and he seemed to be able to almost place the ball in the catcher's mitt.

Williams first played professional baseball with the Texas All-Stars in 1905, then joined the San Antonio Black Bronchos before joining his first top-flight team, the 1911 Lincoln Giants where he made a name for himself by beating Rube Foster in a pitching duel. Over the next five years, Williams reportedly lost only a handful of games. Included in his victories were three games against Major League teams in which he didn't allow a single run.

In his career, Williams won 20 of 27 games against Major Leaguers and his pitching victims included Grover Cleveland Alexander, Rube Marquard, Waite Hoyt, Chief Bender, and Walter Johnson, all Hall of Famers.

Williams was one of the first big drawing cards in the Negro Leagues, and he had several gimmicks that Paige later used, such as constantly lying about his age.

Williams who, according to some, could throw harder than Bob Feller or "Satchel" Paige, averaged well over 10 strikeouts a game for nearly 25 years. His fastball was described in several creative ways: like a pebble in a windstorm, an aspirin tablet with a tail on it, and one catcher claimed that it almost caught fire as it hummed toward the plate. He also was known to throw an emery ball with devastating effectiveness.

In 1925, Williams joined Cum Posey and the Homestead Grays, and although he was 40 years old, some of his greatest games were yet to come. In 1929, he threw one of his many lifetime no-hitters, this one against the General Tires team of Akron, Ohio, featuring Major and Minor League players.

In 1930, under the Kansas City Monarchs' portable lighting system, Williams dueled with Monarchs' pitcher Chet Brewer for 12 innings. Brewer struck out 19, but Williams struck out 27 and allowed only one hit as the Grays won, 1-0.

In 1931, the Grays fielded what is considered by many to be the greatest black team in history. Williams led a pitching staff that included Willie Foster, "Double Duty" Radcliffe, Lefty Williams, Porter Charleston, and George "Chippy" Britt. The Grays won 136 of 155 games and capped the season by demolishing a Major League All-Star team by scores of 10-7 and 18-0.

"[Williams] was over 50 but could still throw 100 miles an hour," recalled "Double Duty" Radcliffe, "I had to put a beefsteak in my glove when I caught him."

Cum Posey named Williams to his post season All-Star team on a pitching staff with Radcliffe, Foster, "Satchel" Paige, Sam Streeter, Charles Beverly, and Pud Flourney, all of whom were at least 15 years Williams' junior.

In the famous 1952 *Pittsburgh Courier* poll, Williams was named the best pitcher in Negro League history, beating out "Satchel" Paige by a single vote.

Right: Before Satchel there was "Smokey" Joe Williams, a hero to thousands of black youngsters.

Appendices

Appendix 1

American teams on which blacks played prior to integration.

Key
ANL = American Negro League
BSP = Black Semipro
BT = Black Traveling
CIL = Chicago Industrial League
ECL = Eastern Colored League
LCBBP = League of Colored Baseball Players
MI = Michigan-Indiana League
NAA = Negro American Association
NAL = Negro American League
NNL2 = Second Negro National League
NNL = Orginal Negro National League
NSL = Negro Southern League
PB = Palm Beach Association
SBL = Southern Baseball League
SLCB = Southern League of Colored Baseball
SNL = Southern Negro League
TNL = Texas Negro League
USL = United States League
WCNL = West Coast Negro Baseball League
WSP = White Semipro teams on which blacks played

A

Abram's Giants Baseball Club (1912, BSP)
African Zulu Giants (1941, BSP)
Akron Black Tyrites (1933, NNL)
Albany Black Senators (1945, BSP)

Albany Black Sox (1937, BSP)
Albany Giants (1926, NSL)
All-American Black Tourists (1907, BT)
Alogoa, Iowa Brownies (1903–1904, BT)
Amarillo Black Sandies (1903, BSP)
Asheville Blues (1940s, NSL)
Atlanta Black Crackers (1920, SNL)
Atlanta Black Crackers (1926, NSL)
Atlanta Black Crackers (1932, NSL)
Atlanta Black Crackers (1938, NAL)
Atlanta Black Crackers (1945, NSL)
Atlanta Braves (1940s, BSP)
Atlanta Genuine Parts (1940s, BSP)
Atlanta Linen Red Sox (1940s, BSP)
Atlantic City Bacharach Giants (1923–28, ECL)
Atlantic City Bacharach Giants (1929, ANL)
Atlantic City Bacharach Giants (1934, NNL)
Austin Black Senators (1929, TNL)

B

Baltimore Black Sox (1932, EWL)
Baltimore Black Sox (1933-34, NNL)
Baltimore Black Sox (1923-28, ECL)
Baltimore Black Sox (1929, ANL)
Baltimore Elite Giants (1938–51, NNL)
Baltimore Lords (1887, LCBC)
Ben Taylor All-Stars (1922, BSP)
Bertha, MN Fisherman (1920s, WSP)
Bibbs Fast Blacks (1940s, BSP)
Birmingham Black Barons (1920, SNL)
Birmingham Black Barons (1923–25, NNL)
Birmingham Black Barons (1926, NSL)
Birmingham Black Barons (1927–30, NNL)
Birmingham Black Barons (1932, NSL)
Birmingham Black Barons (1937–38, NAL)
Birmingham Black Barons (1940–55, NAL)
Birmingham Giants (1904, BSP)
Bismarck Barons (1950s, WSP)
Bismarck Churchills (1930s, WSP)
Black Indians (1930s, BT)
Blue Shadow Blues (1940s, SP)
Bluff City Tigers of Memphis (1910, BSP)
Boston Colored Wolverines (1940s, BSP)
Boston Resolutes (1887, LCBBP)
Boston Royal Giants (1940s, BSP)
Bowser's ABCs (1917, BSP)
Bozzi Stars (1941, BSP)
Broadway Clowns (1940s, BSP)

Bronx Brown Bombers (1937, BSP)

Bronx Giants (1920s, BSP)

Brooklyn All-Stars (1914, BSP)

Brooklyn Brown Dodgers (1945, USL)

Brooklyn Eagles (1935, NNL)

Brooklyn Royal Giants (1923–27, ECL)

Brooklyn Royal Giants (1930s, SP)

Brown Cubs (1920s, BSP)

Brown's Tennessee Rats (BT, 1900s)

Buck Ewing's Stars (1946–1947, BT)

Buffalo Pittsburgh Stars (1920s, BT)

C

California Stars (1930, BSP)

Camp Wheeler Black Spokes (1940s, BSP)

Capital City of Washington (1887, LCBC)

Capital Citys (1887, LCBBP)

Cavalry Detachment Baseball Club (1910, BSP)

Chappie Johnson's Philadelphia Colored Stars
    (1922–23, BSP)

Chappie Johnson's Stars (1929–36, BSP)

Charleston Fultons (1886, SLCB)

Charlotte Black Hornets (1940s, NSL)

Chatam All-Stars (BSP)

Chattanooga All-Stars (1940s, BT)

Chattanooga Black Lookouts (1920, SNL)

Chattanooga Black Lookouts (1930s, NSL)

Chattanooga Choo Choos (1945–1948, NSL)

Chattanooga White Sox (1926, NSL)

Chicago American Giants (1920–31, NNL)

Chicago American Giants (1937–52, NAL)

Chicago Barons (1945, BSP)

Chicago Black Sox (1915, BSP)

Chicago Brown Bombers (1945, BSP)

Chicago Brown Bombers (1945, USL)

Chicago Colored All-Stars (1940s, SP)

Chicago Columbia Giants (1899–1900, BSP)

Chicago Eclipse (1860s, BT)

Chicago Federals (BT)

Chicago Giants (1920–21, NNL)

Chicago Lelands (1910s, SP)

Chicago Monarchs (1930s–1948, BSP)

Chicago, Milwaukee & St. Paul Railroad Giants (1920s,
    SP)

Chicago-Armour (1940s, CIL)

Chicago-Lake View (1940s, CIL)

Chicago-Phillips (1940s, CIL)

Chicago-Pirates (1940s, CIL)

Chicago-Swift (1940s, CIL)

Chicago-Wilson (1940s, CIL)

Chickey Candy Bars (1930s, BSP)

Cincinnati Browns (1887, LCBBP)

Cincinnati Buckeyes (1942, NAL)

Cincinnati Clowns (1943, NAL)

Cincinnati Cresents (1948, SP)

Cincinnati Cubans (1921, NNL)

Cincinnati Tigers (1937, NAL)

Cincinnati-Indianapolis Clowns (1944–45, NAL)

Claybrook Tigers (1936–1937, SP)

Cleveland All-Nations (1933, SP)

Cleveland Bears (1939–40, NAL)

Cleveland Browns (1924, NNL)

Cleveland Buckeyes (1942, NAL)

Cleveland Buckeyes (1943–48, NAL)

Cleveland Cubs (1931, NSL)

Cleveland Elites (1926, NNL)

Cleveland Giants (1933, NNL)

Cleveland Hornets (1927, NNL)

Cleveland Red Sox (1934, NNL)

Cleveland Stars (1932, EWL)

Cleveland Tate Stars (1920s, NNL)

Cleveland Tate Stars (1922, NNL)

Cleveland Tigers (1911, BSP)

Cleveland Tigers (1928, NNL)

Cloverdale Grays (BT)

Cole's American Giants (1932–1933, NSL)

Cole's American Giants (1933–35, NNL)

Cole's American Giants (1934–1935, NNL)

Colored House of David (1930s, SP)

Columbus Blue Birds (1933, NNL)

Columbus Buckeyes (1921, NNL)

Columbus Elite Giants (1935, NNL)

Columbus Turfs (1932, NSL)

Crookston, MN (1930s, WSP)

Cuban All-Stars (1913, BT)

Cuban House of David (1930s, BT)

Cuban Stars (1906, ILIP)

Cuban Stars East (1923–28, ECL)

Cuban Stars East (1929, ANL)

Cuban Stars East (1932, EWL)

Cuban X-Giants (1897–1907, BSP)

D

Dallas Black Cats (1940s, BSP)

Dallas Black Giants (1929, TNL)

Dallas Longview Giants (1910s, BSP)

Danville Giants (1900s, BT)
Danville Unions (1900s, BT)
Danville, IL Browns (1909, BSP)
Dayton Chappies (1917, BSP)
Dayton Marcos (1920s, NNL)
Dayton Monarchs (1930s, BSP)
Dayton Shrovers (1930s, BSP)
Denison Hotel Club Scrappers (1890s, BSP)
Denver Trojans (1940s, BSP)
Denver White Elephants (1930s–40s, BSP)
Detroit Colored Giants (1940s, BSP)
Detroit Giants (1934, BT)
Detroit Motor City Giants (1945, USL)
Detroit Stars (1920–31, NNL)
Detroit Stars (1937, NAL)
Detroit Stars (1954–55, NAL)
Detroit Wolves (1932, EWL)
Dick Jones's ABCs (1935, BSP)
Dismukes' Valley Tigers (1931, BT)
Dizzy Dismukes All-Stars (1920s)
Dunseith Acme Colored Giants (1930s, SP)

E

East Chicago Giants (1930–1950, BSP)
East St. Louis Imperials (1900s, BSP)
Edgewater Giants (1941, BSP)
Elkhart Giants (1930s, BSP)
Ethiopian Clowns (1930s–40s, SP)
Evansville Colored Braves (1930s, BSP)

F

Fall City of Louisiana (1887, LCBC)
Fall Citys (1887, LCBBP)
Farley Stars (1940s, SP)
Florida Clippers (1886, SLCB)
Florida Colored Hoboes (1940s, BT)
Florida Stars (1927, BT)
Fort Jackson Blue Sox (1940s, BSP)
Fort Worth Black Cats (1929, TNL)
Fort Worth Yellow Jackets (1910s, BSP)
Freeman Nine (1890s, BT)
French Lick Plutos (1910s, BSP)
French Lick Red Devils (1900s, BSP)

G

Georgia Champions (1886, SLCB)
Georgia Indians (1940s, BSP)
Georgia Sunshine Stars (1940s, BSP)

Gilkerson's Union Giants (1920–1935, BT)
Grass Skirts (1940s, SP)
Greathouse Giants (1930s, BSP)
Greenlee's Crawfords (1945, USL)
Greenville Delta Giants (1950, BSP)

H

Harlem Globetrotters (1945–1949, SP)
Harlem Stars (1930s, BSP)
Harrisburg Black Sox (1940s, BSP)
Harrisburg Giants (1924–27, ECL)
Harrisburg-St.Louis Stars (1943, NNL)
Havana Cuban Giants (1930s, BT)
Havana Stars (1906, BT)
Hilldale Daisies of Darby, PA (1916–1922, BSP)
Hilldale Daisies of Darby, PA (1923–1928, ECL)
Hilldale Daisies of Darby, PA (1929, ANL)
Hilldale Daisies of Darby, PA (1930–1931, BSP)
Hilldale Daisies of Darby, PA (1932, EWL)
Hilldale Giants (1945, USL)
Homestead Grays (1929, ANL)
Homestead Grays (1930, NNL)
Homestead Grays (1932, EWL)
Homestead Grays (1933, NNL)
Homestead Grays (1935–37, NNL)
Houston Black Buffaloes (1929, TNL)
Houston Black Buffaloes (1940s, NSL)
Houston Eagles (1949–1950s, NAL)

I

Idaho Stars (1930s, BT)
Illinois Giants (1919–1929, BT)
Illinois Giants of Danville (1910s, BT)
Indianapolis ABC's (1920–26, NNL)
Indianapolis ABC's (1931, NNL)
Indianapolis ABC's (1932, NSL)
Indianapolis ABC's (1933, NNL)
Indianapolis ABC's (1938–39, NAL)
Indianapolis Athletics (1937, NAL)
Indianapolis Clowns (1946–60, NAL)
Indianapolis Eagles (1867, BT)
Indianapolis Mohawks (1867, BT)
Indianapolis Monarchs (1930s, BSP)
Indianapolis X-ABCs (1916, BT)
Indianapolis-Cincinnati Clowns (1944–45, NAL)
Indianapolis-Toledo Crawfords(1939–40, NAL)

J

Jacksonville Athletics (1886, SLCB)
Jacksonville Macedonias (1886, SLCB)
Jacksonville Red Caps (1920, SNL)
Jacksonville Red Caps (1930s–1940s, NAL, BSP)
Jacksonville Red Caps (1938, NAL)
Jacksonville Red Caps (1941–42, NAL)
Jamestown Red Sox (1930s, WSP)
Jersey City Colored Athletics (1910s, SP)
Jersey City Giants (1924, BSP)
Jeweler's ABCs (BSP)
Joe Louis All-Stars (1940s, BT)
Johnny Baker Colored Giants (1920s, SP)

K

Kansas City All-Nations (1910s, BT)
Kansas City KS Giants (1910, BT)
Kansas City Monarchs (1920–30, NNL)
Kansas City Monarchs (1932, NSL)
Kansas City Monarchs (1933–1936, BSP)
Kansas City Monarchs (1937–55, NAL)
Kansas City Monarchs All-Stars (1938–1942, BT)
Kansas City Royals (1911, BSP)
Kansas City Royals (1940s, BSP)
Kary All-Stars (1930s, SP)
Kentucky Unions (1909, BSP)
Knoxville Black Smokies (1940s, SBL)
Knoxville Grays (1940s, NSL)
Knoxville Smokies (1945, NSL)

L

League of Colored Baseball Clubs, 1887
Lima-Ohio Colored All-Stars (1940s, BT)
Lincoln Giants (1923–26, ECL)
Lincoln Giants (1927–28, ECL)
Lincoln Giants (1929, ANL)
Little Falls, MN (1920s–1930s, WSP)
Little Rock Black Travelers (1929, TNL)
Little Rock Black Travelers (1945, NSL)
Little Rock Black Travlers (1940s, NSL)
Little Rock Greys (1932, NSL)
Lord Baltimores (1887, LCBBP)
Los Angeles White Sox (1946, WCNBL)
Los Angles White Sox (1920s–1930s, BSP)
Louisville Black Caps (1930)
Louisville Black Caps (1930s, BSP)
Louisville Black Caps (1932, NSL)

Louisville Black Colonels (1930s, BSP)
Louisville Black Colonels (1954, NAL)
Louisville Buckeyes (1949, NAL)
Louisville Tigers (1911, BSP)
Louisville White Caps (1930, NNL)
Louisville White Sox (1931, NNL)

M

Madison Colored Giants (1930s, BT)
Mariana Giants (1910, BSP)
Memphis Eclipses (1886, SLCB)
Memphis Eurekas (1886, SLCB)
Memphis Grey Sox (1940s, SBL)
Memphis Grey Sox (1945, NAL)
Memphis Red Sox (1923–25, NNL)
Memphis Red Sox (1926, NSL)
Memphis Red Sox (1927–30, NNL)
Memphis Red Sox (1932, NSL)
Memphis Red Sox (1937–55, NAL)
Miami Giants (1930s, BSP)
Michigan City Wonders (1910s, BSP)
Michigan City Wonders (1930, BSP)
Milwaukee Bears (1923, NNL)
Minneapolis Colored Keystones (1911, BSP)
Minneapolis Keystones (1900s, BSP)
Minneapolis-St. Paul Gophers (1945, NAL)
Minneola, TX Black Spiders (BT, 1900s)
Minot Mallards (1950s, WSP)
Minnesota Keystones (1910, BSP)
Mobile Black Bears (1945, NSL)
Mobile Black Shippers (1940s, SBL)
Mobile Brooklyns (1920s, BSP)
Mohawk Giants of Schenectady, NY (1912–1941, BSP)
Monroe Monarchs (1930s, NSL)
Montgomery Blues (1886, SLCB)
Montgomery Gray Sox (1916, 1940s)
Montgomery Gray Sox (1921, NSL)
Montgomery Gray Sox (1940s, NSL)
Montgomery Grey Sox(1932, NSL)
Montgomery Grey Sox (1926, NSL)
Moss Point Giants of Mississippi (1910, BT)
Mound City Blues (1938, BSP)
Muskogee Cardinals (1948, BSP)

N

Nashville Black Vols (1940s, NSL)
Nashville Black Vols (1940s, SBL)

Nashville Elite Giants (1926, NSL)
Nashville Elite Giants (1930, NNL)
Nashville Elite Giants (1932, NSL)
Nashville Elite Giants (1933–34, NNL)
Nashville Giants (1920, SNL)
Nashville Standard Giants (1910, BSP)
Nebraska Full-Blooded Indians (1906)
New Orleans Armstrongs (1930s, BSP)
New Orleans Black Pelicans (1920, SNL)
New Orleans Black Pelicans (1940s, NSL)
New Orleans Black Pelicans (1940s, SBL)
New Orleans Creole (1940s, BSP)
New Orleans Eagles (1951, NAL)
New Orleans Unions (1886, SLCB)
New Orleans-St.Louis Stars (1941, NAL)
New Rockford, ND (1930s, WSP)
New York Black Yankees (1932, EWL)
New York Black Yankees (1933–1936, BSP)
New York Black Yankees (1937–48, NNL)
New York Colored Giants (1910, BT)
New York Cubans (1887, LCBBP)
New York Cubans (1935–36, NNL)
New York Cubans (1939–50, NNL)
New York Gorhams (1887, LCBBP)
New York Gothams (1887, LCBC)

New York Red Caps (1919, BSP)
Newark Browns (1932, EWL)
Newark Dodgers (1934–35, NNL)
Newark Eagles (1936–48, NNL)
Newark Stars (1926, ECL)
Norfolk Red Stockings (1920s, BSP)
Norfolk Royals (1948, NAA)
Norfolk Stars (1920–1921, BSP)

O
Oakland Larks (1940s, WCNL)
Oklahoma Monarchs (1910, BT)
Oklahoma City Black Indians (1930s, BSP)
Original Mohawk Giants of Schenectady (1913–1915, BSP)

P
Palmer House Stars (1940s, BSP)
Park City Grays of Bowling Green, KY (1910, BSP)
Pekin Tigers of Cincinnati (1913, BT)
Pensacola Giants (1912, BSP)
Peoria Black Devils (1920, BT)
Philadelphia Giants (1906, ILIP)
Philadelphia Giants (1929, ANL)
Philadelphia Giants (1932, EWL)
Philadelphia Hilldales (1945, USL)
Philadelphia Professionals (1906, ILIP)
Philadelphia Pythians (1887, LCBBP)
Philadelphia Stars (1933–52, NNL)

Below: In 1961, Calvin Griffith moved the Washington Senators to Minnesota because there were less black fans, but his stars in the Twin Cities were Tony Oliva (back row, right) and Rod Carew (front row, second from left).

Philadelphia Tigers (1928, ECL)
Pittsburgh Crawfords (1920s, BSP)
Pittsburgh Crawfords (1932, EWL)
Pittsburgh Crawfords (1933–38, NNL)
Pittsburgh Crawfords (1945, USL)
Pittsburgh Keystones (1887, LCBBP)
Pittsburgh Keystones (1922, NNL)
Pittsburgh Monarchs (1940s, BSP)
Portland Rosebuds (1946, WCNL)
Portsmouth Black Sox (1930s, BT)

Q

Quaker Giants (1906, ILIP)

R

Renville, MN (1905, BSP)
Richmond Giants (1948, NAA)
Richmond Paramounts (1930s, BSP)
Riverton-Palmyra Athletics (1906, ILIP)
Rocky Hill Tigers (1920s, BSP)
Roman Cities (1886, SLCB)
Royal Poinciana (1890–1920, PB)

S

San Antonio Black Aces (1910s, TNL)
San Antonio Black Indians (1929, TNL)
San Antonio Broncos (1907, BSP)
San Francisco Sea Lions (1940s, WCNL)
Satchel Paige All-Stars (1930s–1940s, BT)
Savannah Broads (1886, SLCB)
Savannah Jerseys (1886, SLCB)
Savannah Lafayettes (1886, SLCB)
Schenectady Black Sox (1937, BSP)
Schenectady Royal Giants (1946, BSP)
Scripto Black Cats (1940s, BSP)
Seattle Steelheads (1946, WCNBL)
Shreveport Black Sports (1929, TNL)
Silver Moons (1931, BSP)
South Bend ABCs (1913, BSP)
South Bend Hoosier Beers (1949, WSP)
South Bend Studebaker Athletics (1948, WSP)
St. Louis Black Sox (1909, BSP)
St. Louis Giants (1920–21, NNL)
St. Louis Stars (1922–31, NNL)
St. Louis Stars (1937, NAL)
St. Louis Stars (1939, NAL)
St. Louis-Harrisburg Stars (1943, NAL)
St. Louis-New Orleans Stars (1941, NAL)

St. Paul Colored Giants (1907–1908, BSP)
St. Paul Colored Gophers (1915, BSP)
Stillwater, OK Tigers (1930s, BSP)
Sudan Black Cats (1910s, BSP)
Sunshine Babies (1928, BT)
Swift Black Cats (1940s, BSP)

T

Tampa Pepsi-Cola Giants (1940s, SP)
Tappin, Virginia Spartans (1910s, BSP)
Taylor ABCs (1920–1931, BSP)
Taylor's Indianapolis ABCs (1916, BSP)
Terre Haute Giants (1913, BSP)
Toledo Crawfords (1939–1941, NAL)
Toledo Rays (1890, BSP)
Toledo Rays (1945, USL)
Toledo Tigers (1923, NNL)
Toledo Tigers (1923, NNL)
Toledo-Indianapolis Crawfords (1939–40, NAL)
Troy Colored Giants (1941, BSP)
Twin Cities Colored Giants (1934–1936, BT)
Twin City Gophers (1911, BSP)

V

Valley City, ND (1930s, WSP)

W

Washington Black Senators (1938, NNL)
Washington Elite Giants (1935–37, NNL)
Washington-Philadelphia Pilots (1930s, BT)
Washington Pilots (1932, EWL)
Washington Potomacs (1924, ECL)
Washington-Homestead Grays (1937–48, NNL)
West Baden Sprudels (1913–1915, BSP)
Wichita Falls Black Spudders (1929, TNL)
Wilmington Giants (1906, ILIP)
Wilmington Potomacs (1925, ECL)
Wilmington Royal Blues (1920s, BSP)
Winona Merchants (1930s, WSP)
Winston-Salem Eagles (1938, BSP)
World's All-Nations (1910s, BT)

Y

York Monarchs (1890, BSP)

Z

Zulu Cannibal Giants (1930s–1948, BSP)

Appendix 2

MAJOR LEAGUE MANAGERS OF COLOR

Frank Robinson: 1975–77 Cleveland Indians, 1981–1984 San Francisco Giants, 1988–1991 Baltimore Orioles, 2002 Montreal Expos
Larry Doby: 1978 Chicago White Sox
Maury Wills: 1980–1981 Seattle Mariners
Cito Gaston: 1989–1997 Toronto Blue Jays
Hal McRae: 1991–1994 Kansas City Royals, 2001–2002 Tampa Bay Devil Rays
Felipe Alou: 1992–2001 Montreal Expos
Tony Perez: 1993 Cincinnati Reds, 2001 Florida Marlins
Dusty Baker: 1993–2002 San Francisco Giants, 2003 Chicago Cubs
Don Baylor: 1993–1998 Colorado Rockies, 2000–2002 Chicago Cubs
Jerry Manuel: 1998–2003 Chicago White Sox
Davey Lopes: 2000–2002 Milwaukee Brewers
Lloyd McClendon: 2001–2003 Pittsburgh Pirates
Jerry Royster: 2002 Milwaukee Brewers
Luis Pujols: 2002 Detroit Tigers
Tony Pena: 2002–2003 Kansas City Royals
Omar Minaya: 2003 Montreal Expos

MAJOR LEAGUE GENERAL MANAGERS OF COLOR

Bill Lucas: 1979 Atlanta Braves
Bob Watson: 1994–1995 Houston Astros, 1996–1997 New York Yankees
Ken Williams: 2002–2003 Chicago White Sox

MAJOR LEAGUE EXECUTIVES OF COLOR

Jimmie Lee Solomon: Senior Vice President of Baseball Operations
Jonathan Mariner: Chief Financial Officer of Major League Baseball
Bob Watson: Major League Baseball's Vice President in charge of discipline
Hank Aaron: Senior Vice President, Atlanta Braves

MAJOR LEAGUE OWNERS OF COLOR

Ulice Payne: President, Milwaukee Brewers

Appendix 3

ESTIMATED LIFETIME TOTALS OF "THE LEGENDS"

Note: These totals are estimates based on available statistics in conjunction with conjecture on the actual number of games played against all competition. A majority of games played by Negro Leaguers were against white semipro teams not of Major League caliber. In no way are these totals intended to "prove" that a certain Negro Leaguer was as good or better than another Major Leaguer —it's like comparing apples to oranges. The most startling things about these statistics are the sheer size of the numbers, for Negro Leaguer players usually played year-round, and had careers much longer than the average Major Leaguer. Pete Rose, for example, is the all-time Major League leader in games with 3562. If Rose's Minor League career and exhibitions are added he would have about 4000 games. There were dozens of Negro Leaguers who played more games than Rose.

(See table on page 175)

WL WIN PERCENTAGE:

"Satchel" Paige 750, 150, .833
Hilton Smith 365, 95, .793
Leon Day 330, 105, .759
Martin Dihigo 280, 140, .667
"Bullet" Rogan 255, 95, .729
Willie Foster 250, 100, .714
Rube Foster 210, 70, .750

Players	Games	ABs	Hits	HRs	Avg.	SBs
Josh Gibson	3,000	13,800	5,175	926	.375	200
Buck Leonard	3,400	15,300	5,584	700	.360	150
"Pop" Lloyd	4,500	19,800	7,029	330	.355	500
Oscar Charleston	4,200	17,600	6,160	519	.350	700
Willie Wells	4,200	18,900	6,520	275	.345	650
"Cool Papa" Bell	3,750	18,000	6,210	320	.345	2,000
"Turkey" Stearnes	3,000	12,600	4,221	796	.335	350
"Bullet" Rogan	4,000	16,000	5,200	370	.325	200
Ray Dandridge	3,000	13,200	4,092	220	.310	250
Martin Dihigo	3,300	15,000	4,575	611	.305	300
Judy Johnson	2,500	10,000	2,850	120	.285	300
Monte Irvin★	764	2,499	731	99	.293	28
Jackie Robinson★	1,382	4,877	1,518	137	.311	197

★Major League totals only

Sources:

Websites
www.baseball-almanac.com; www.baseball-reference.com

Books
Aaron, Hank with Lonnie Wheeler, *I Had a Hammer*, Harper Collins, 1991.

Bak, Richard, *Turkey Stearnes and the Detroit Stars*, Wayne State University Press, 1994.

Bruce, Janet, *The Kansas City Monarchs—Champions of Baseball*, University Press of Kansas, 1985.

Holway, John B., *Blackball Stars*, New York, Carroll & Graf Publishers/Richard Gallen, 1988.

Johnson, Lloyd and Wolff, Miles, ed., *The Baseball Encyclopedia of Minor League Baseball*, Durham, NC: Baseball America, 1993.

Lester, Larry, *Black Baseball's National Showcase*, Lincoln, NE: University of Nebraska Press, 2001.

McNary, Kyle P., *Ted 'Double Duty' Radcliffe—36 Years of Pitching & Catching in Baseball's Negro Leagues*, Minneapolis: McNary Pub., 1994.

Paige, Satchel and Lipman, David, *Maybe I'll Pitch Forever*, University of Nebraska Press, 1993.

Peterson, Robert, *Only the Ball was White*, Grammercy, 1999.

Reichler, Joseph L., ed., *The Baseball Encyclopedia* 4th ed., rev., New York: Macmillan, 1979.

Robinson, Jackie and Duckett, Alfred, *I Never Had it Made*, New York: Harper Collins, 1972.

Riley, James A., *The Biographical Enclyclopedia of the Negro Baseball Leagues*, Carroll & Graf, 2002.

White, Sol, *Official Base Ball Guide*, Columbia, SC: Camden House, 1984.

Articles
"The Story of Marvelous Rube Foster," *Afro Magazine*, (September 5, 1953), 6.

"A Black Man in the Wigwam," *Ebony Magazine*, (February, 1969), 66–7.

Personal Interviews
Norman Lumpkin, Sr., Double Duty Radcliffe, Bobby Robinson, Lester Lockett, Sam Hairston, Louis Clarizio, Garnett Blair, Maceo Breedlove, Sherwood Brewer, Wilmer Fields, Saul Davis, Leon Day, Josh Johnson, Buck Leonard, Buck O'Neil, Bob Feller, Will Owen, Pullman Porter, Merle Porter, Red Moore, Elmer Knox, Rev. Butler, Piper Davis, George Jefferson, Maurice Peatros, Slick Surratt, and Lyman Bostock.

Index